Sarah Dodd is the founding owner of Tree Law Ltd, a law firm specialising in the claims involving trees.

Prior to setting up Tree Law, Sarah carried out her training contract with the NHS in Wales, qualifying as a solicitor in January 2002. On qualification Sarah moved to work at Eversheds where she acted for insurance companies, utility providers and banks in relation to their civil claims. She moved from there to DACBeachcroft where she led the subsidence team acting for numerous household insurers, later becoming a partner.

In 2018 Sarah took on the role as Vice Chair of the Industry Subsidence Forum and became the Chair from 2020 until 2022. Sarah has been part of the team involved in the redraft of the London Tree Officers' Joint Mitigation Protocol, which is due to launch in 2025 for use in subsidence claims.

Tree Law was launched in November 2021 following a desire to focus her expertise on tree claims and provide a service putting the environment at the heart of advice. Sarah is now proud to refer call herself The Tree Hugging Lawyer.

A Practical Guide to the Law in Relation to Tree Root Subsidence Claims

A Practical Guide to the Law in Relation to Tree Root Subsidence Claims

Sarah Dodd

Solicitor (England & Wales)

Law Brief Publishing

Published 2025 by Law Brief Publishing, an imprint of Law Brief Publishing Ltd
30 The Parks
Minehead
Somerset
TA24 8BT

www.lawbriefpublishing.com

Paperback: 978-1-918241-05-1

For my Dad

Always my biggest supporter

PREFACE

Subsidence is the downward movement of a property which is caused when the ground beneath the foundations sinks. This volumetric change of the soil can arise from many causes, but this book focuses on one cause in particular, trees.

Tree root induced subsidence is linked to weather conditions. During hot, dry summers, tree roots extract moisture from shrinkable clay soils leading to desiccation, soil shrinkage and subsequent foundation movements. As the UK experiences hotter and drier summers due to climate change, claims arising from tree related subsidence are both increasing in number and are also occurring in parts of the UK which have, until now, been too mild/wet for tree root subsidence.

Resolving tree root subsidence is difficult. Subsidence of the ground will continue until the underlying cause is addressed. To date this has frequently meant identifying if a tree is responsible and felling that tree. But with a growing recognition of the vital role of urban trees, the law and practice around managing tree root subsidence claims are evolving.

Exciting innovations in engineering, stabilising techniques and industry wide protocols are shifting the approach from the tree removal as the default to more nuanced solutions that balance the right of the homeowner, the tree and the community.

The aim of this book is to provide a guide to the law related to tree root subsidence claims. It explains how established legal principles are applied in this specialist context and is intended for the use of all those impacted in such claims from homeowners, insurers, local authorities and the general public.

Except where otherwise indicated, the law and procedure set out in this book are stated as the author understands them to have effect as at 30th September 2025.

Sarah Dodd
September 2025

CONTENTS

CHAPTER ONE

WHAT IS TREE ROOT SUBSIDENCE?

1. Introduction

Before looking at tree root subsidence, this book begins by considering what subsidence damage actually is.

Subsidence is defined by the Financial Ombudsman Service as "the downward movement of the site on which a building stands, where the soil beneath the building's foundations is unstable. This movement can occur due to various factors, including changes in moisture levels or the weight of the building itself."

Tree root (or vegetation related) subsidence is the downward movement of the site on which the building stands caused by the influence of tree roots on the moisture content of the soils underlying the property foundations. Clay soils cause subsidence primarily due to their ability to absorb and release moisture leading to seasonal shrinking and swelling. The soil swells in the winter period as the weather is wetter and trees have a lower water demand and then shrink over the summer as roots take up water from the soil in the course of transpiration.

Where roots from a tree have grown underneath the foundations of a property built on clay shrinkable soil, the drying effect can be enough to cause differential movement of the property. Where the movement is significant enough it can cause windows and doors to 'stick' and cracking to appear. In the worst case scenario, the damage can be significant enough to cause instability of the structure and demolition of a property can be required in rare situations.

Tree root subsidence is wholly linked to our weather. The number of episodes of subsidence damage will be higher after a hot and dry summer. A year with an above average number of these claims is labelled a 'surge' or 'event' year. With climate change impacting the UK, these event years are becoming more common.

2. A history of insurance cover

In the insurance industry subsidence damage is what is known as an 'insured peril', i.e., an event or risk that is covered under an insurance policy.

Subsidence damage has not always been covered as standard by insurance in the UK. As a result of the surge in claims from the summer of 1976 pressure grew on the insurance industry to step in and deal with those claims. Pressures included:

1. The scale of claims – Tens of thousands of properties across the South East of England were affected at once, showing that subsidence was not a niche problem.

2. Public and political pressure – Media coverage of distressed homeowners and MPs raising subsidence as an issue before parliament put the insurance industry under pressure.

3. Consumer expectations – Homeowners who had paid for buildings insurance assumed that it would provide cover for this structural damage.

4. Market competition – Some insurance companies started to offer subsidence cover as standard, leading to market competition.

5. Legal pressure – Policy disputes led to litigation risk for insurance companies.

6. Development on shrinkable soils – The scale of housing development in areas underlain by a clay soil means that this was an issue of increasing risk as more properties were built in subsidence prone areas.

7. Regulatory and industry guidance – The Association of British Insurers began pushing for clearer, fairer treatment of subsidence claims and urging consistency by their insurer members.

8. Risk spreading – Insurers were able to assess and spread the risk to manage their financial exposure using policy excesses, insurance conditions and reinsurance.

From 1976 onwards subsidence has been underwritten by insurers as part of their mainstream buildings insurance offering.

3. Climate Change & Data

The impact of climate change is a growing concern in the area of tree root subsidence.

Tree root subsidence is the only peril which is made worse by climate change and where the traditional approach to remedy a claim can be to fell an implicated tree which, in turn, contributes towards making climate change worse.

In the UK as our summers are getting hotter and drier, the conditions conducive to tree root subsidence risk are becoming more common. As our climate changes, subsidence claims are appearing in parts of the UK which have historically been too mild or wet to experience much tree root subsidence.

Event years are getting more common. Having occurred in 1976, 1983, 1989-1991, 1995, 2003, 2006, 2018, 2022 and with 2025 about to be declared an event year.

In the last surge event of 2022 the Association of British Insurers (ABI) reported 23,000 subsidence claims costing the insurance industry £219m with an average claim cost of £9600. The hot summer of 2025 is yet to be declared an event year (as at the time of writing) but this looks likely. This surge however sees an increase in the average spend per claim up to over £17,000 as the higher cost of materials impacts insurance claim cost.

4. Insurance risk profiling and postcode analysis

Insurance companies assess risk by using data relating to past claims. Reflecting back on data where we are moving forward in a changing climate can risk making inaccurate assessments.

Increasingly insurance companies are relying on a variety of sources of data to assess subsidence risk. From soil and geology maps, met office climate data, historical claims data, remote sensing and satellite imagery, tree and vegetation databased, property age and construction type, water company data and geospatial risk tools.

These sources can come together in a postcode-based assessment. Properties in 'high risk' areas, such as parts of North London, Surrey and Kent can be deemed a high risk due to a number of factors being present which might make a property prone to subsidence damage. In those areas higher insurance premiums may be charged to reflect the insurance risk. In other cases, policies may not be offered to properties given their risk level.

Whilst I cannot credit this statistic to a particular industry expert, it is accepted that even in the highest risk areas, no property has more than a 5% chance of suffering from subsidence damage due to a tree. In the industry others have commented that 5% is a generous figure and actually this % risk is far closer to a 1 or 2% chance.

Due to a reliance on data, there is a fast-emerging industry in modelling and data to help and support insurance companies in this assessment.

Not only can this data help insurance companies but it is also of interest to property buyers. This data allows buyers to make informed decisions on risk when buying a property and to the mortgage industry focused on maintaining the value of the property against which their mortgage loan is secured.

5. The role of insurers and their supply chain

When a homeowner notices crack damage to their property and makes a claim on their insurance policy, the claim is typically managed by the insurance company's specialist suppliers. There are a number of such suppliers in the industry who provide a subsidence specific service to insurance companies, manage the claim from its first notification stage (FNOL) through to conclusion, and even legal recovery claim.

In broad terms the claim process follows these key steps:

- First notification of loss – Claim notified by the homeowner to the insurer and the insurer instructs one of their suppliers

- Initial assessment – The supplier carries out their initial assessment of the damage to start the process of verifying whether the damage is subsidence and whether the claim should be accepted under the policy.

- Site investigations – A suite of site investigations are carried out in order to determine the soil type and condition and the presence or not of roots under the foundations. Drainage investigation will also be carried out to rule out leaking drains as a cause of the subsidence.

- Monitoring – The property can be monitored by way of crack monitoring or level monitoring and distortion survey. The purpose of monitoring being to review the pattern of movement of the property, with the up (winter) and down (summer) pattern being indicative of the influence of vegetation.

- Remote investigation – The Covid pandemic, the increase in reliance on remote/satellite technology and the ability to tap into a data banks from past claims is seeing the increase in remote site investigations and analysis.

- Arboricultural assessment – Where investigations indicate that the property has suffered damage as a result of the impact of vegetation, an arboricultural investigation will go ahead to assess which trees might be implicated in the damage.

Once this evidence has been gathered, the insurers will be able to review the conclusions of their supplier and insurance cover will either be accepted or rejected.

If the claim is accepted under the subsidence peril the claim moves to the next stage: mitigation (Chapter 3).

CHAPTER TWO

NUISANCE AND NEGLIGENCE

Legal claims arising from tree root subsidence damage are tortious civil claims, progressed under the laws of nuisance and negligence.

1. Negligence

The foundations of negligence were set out in *Donoghue v Stevenson*[1] by the House of Lords. The 'neighbour principle' is that you must take reasonable care to avoid acts or omissions which you can reasonably foresee would be likely to injure your 'neighbour'. Your neighbour being 'persons who are so closely and directly affected by your act that you ought reasonably to have them in contemplation when you are directing your mind to the acts or omissions in question.'

So, when applying that to tree root subsidence cases, a landowner should take care not to use their land, or fail to manage their land, in a way that causes foreseeable harm to their neighbour. The neighbour in this scenario most commonly being an adjoining property owner.

To succeed in proving negligence the core principles have to be established, namely:

- **Duty of Care** – The tree owner owed a duty to take reasonable care not to cause foreseeable harm

[1] Donoghue v Stevenson [1932] AC 562

- **Breach** – The tree owner fell below the standard of the reasonable person in their actions

- **Causation** – The breach is the cause of damage

- **Damage** – The claimant suffers a loss (which is not too remote)

2. Private Nuisance

Private nuisance is an unlawful and unreasonable interference with someone's use or enjoyment of their land, or with their rights over land.

This can be physical damage to the land itself, such as subsidence damage or direct root damage (when the root itself causes physical damage such as to pavements and walls). It can also be an interference with the reasonable enjoyment and amenity of the land from encroaching branches.

Private nuisance is defined in Clerk & Lindsell on Torts[2] as "the continuous unlawful and indirect interference with the use of enjoyment of land, or of some right over or in connection with it".

3. Delaware Mansions

The case of *Delaware Mansions v Westminster City Council*[3] is a cornerstone in tree root subsidence litigation. In this case the House of Lords addressed how the law treats both nuisance and negligence in tree root subsidence claims.

---

2 Clerk & Lindsell on Torts (24th edn, Sweet & Maxwell 2023)

3 Delaware Mansions v Westminster City Council [2001] UKHL 55

Delaware Mansions is a block of mansion flats in Maida Vale, London. The tree in question was a large London Plane tree on the pavement outside the flats, owned and managed by Westminster City Council. In the late 1970s cracks appeared in the mansion flats. Investigations concluded that this was because the tree's roots were drawing moisture from the clay subsoil underneath the property foundations. The damage had begun when the property was owned by the Church Commissioners and the freehold was later purchased by Delaware Mansions Ltd. Delaware Mansions complained to Westminster about the damage and asked them to abate the nuisance. No abatement work was carried out. To stabilise the property, Delaware carried out underpinning works, taking the depth of the foundations down to ground beneath the influence of the tree's roots. Delaware then brought the legal claim against Westminster to recover the cost of that underpinning work.

The key legal points that come from this case are:

1. Nuisance and not negligence was the correct cause of action.

2. Liability only arose once the council knew, or ought to have known, of the damage and failed to act reasonably;

3. Even though some damage pre-dated Delaware Mansion's ownership, they were still able to recover reasonable remedial costs because the nuisance was continuing when they took over the freehold.

In particular, around the issue of whether nuisance or negligence was the correct cause of action, the House of Lords said nuisance is the right cause of action in tree root subsidence cases. As such, liability starts once the tree owner knows, or ought to know, of the damage and fails to act. So even though in this case the damage had begun before the Council were on notice, the duty to abate the nuisance arose once knowledge existed and continued thereafter.

The freeholders were therefore able to recover the reasonable costs of remedial works as damages in the claim in nuisance.

4. Foreseeability

In both negligence and nuisance, liability rests on foreseeability.

The starting point on foreseeability is the case of *Cambridge Water Co v Eastern Counties Leather*[4] which is a House of Lords decision in a contamination case. That set out the principle that foreseeability of the type of damage is essential. If the kind of harm could not reasonably have been foreseen then there can be no liability.

Foreseeability has become a significant focus in tree root subsidence litigation since the case of *Berent v Family Mosaic Housing*.[5]

In the case of Berent the property was house in Islington owned by Ms Berent. The trees implicated were a London Plane tree owned by Islington Council and other trees owned by the housing association, Family Mosaic Housing. Cracks started to appear at the property in 2003. Expert evidence obtained concluded that the property was damaged by tree root subsidence from the nearby trees. Both Islington and Family Mosaic were put on notice of the damage and had been asked to carry out tree removal or tree pruning as a way of abating the nuisance. That work was not done and so the property was underpinned.

A legal claim was brought against both Islington Council and Family Mosaic Housing in both nuisance and negligence. The claim was for damages to reimburse the cost of the underpinning and remedial work to the property.

---

4 Cambridge Water Co v Eastern Counties Leather [1994] 2AC 264

5 Berent v Family Mosaic Housing [2012] EWCA Civ 961.

In the defence of this claim both defendants argued that the crack damage was not caused by the trees but other factors, and also argued that they had not acted unreasonably.

The trial Judge found in favour of the defendants, concluding that the evidence did not show that, on the balance of probabilities, the tree had caused the damage. This was appealed by the claimant to the Court of Appeal who upheld the trial Judge's decision and said that the claimant's expert evidence was not strong enough to show causation.

The Court of Appeal addressed the issue of foreseeability which has become a key in tree root subsidence litigation. The Court of Appeal said that in both nuisance and negligence foreseeability of damage is a prerequisite for liability. The Court of Appeal found that the risk of tree root subsidence damage was not foreseeable. In considering foreseeability all of the facts of the situation needed to be considered. The size of the tree, shrinkability of the soil, the proximity of the tree to the house and the history in relation to this type of damage.

In this case foreseeability was not established as the tree was relatively small, the soil was not highly shrinkable and there had been no prior indication of problems.

Since the Berent case, case law that has followed has added some clarification to the issue of foreseeability.

Khan & Khan v Harrow Council & Kane[6] was a case before the Technology and Construction Court. In this case the claimants owned a house in Harrow. There were two sets of vegetation of relevance in their claim, a tall Lawson Cypress hedge, 10 metres high and just half a metre from the site of the claimants' property. This belonged to Ms Kane. The other was a mature Oak tree, further away and belonging to the Harrow Council. The claim was brought against both the next-

---

6 Khan & Khan v Harrow Council & Kane [2013] EWHC 2687

door neighbour and the Council. On foreseeability the key issue was whether the defendants could reasonably have foreseen that their vegetation posed a risk of this kind (tree root subsidence).

The Court's decision was that the Cypress hedge owned by the next-door neighbour was extremely close to the house and was unusually tall. The Court found that it was foreseeable to any reasonable landowner that this tree could cause damage. Therefore, Mrs Kane was liable in nuisance. The Oak tree was further way and the Court held that the Council could not have foreseen the risk of subsidence from it and so the claim against the Council failed.

The key point made by the Khan case was that foreseeability is judged objectively. It is about what a reasonably prudent landowner would not and not what that particular defendant knew.

The case of *Pattichis v London Borough of Enfield*[7] was important in showing that historic subsidence incidents involving the same tree can be used to establish foreseeability in future claims as part of a 'hot spot' argument. Whilst there is no clear set of rules as to what classes as a historic subsidence incident, reasonableness will likely be applied here. Past claims being those where a payment of damages was made by the local authority, potentially over a certain amount of money, in relation to a claim involving the same type of tree and in close proximity to the property in the subject claim.

These cases have therefore created the following ways of establishing foreseeability:

1. Where there had been a prior subsidence claim involving the same tree and the same property and where a damages payment was made and, potentially the requested tree works had not been carried out;

[7] Pattichis v London Borough of Enfield [2016] TCC

2. Where the tree was a 'real risk' – i.e., a tree so large and/or close to the property and/or unusual in its type that it was unique and would have been enough to put a reasonable landowner on notice of the risk of it causing damage

3. The notion of a 'hot spot' area – this is something of relevance to local authority tree owners and relates to where there is an area known to be common for tree root subsidence claims.

5. Causation

Causation feels like the heart of a legal claim. This is often the part of the legal tests that clients can misunderstand as being the only element that determines whether a claim succeeds or fails. Whereas a tree can be the cause of damage but the tree owner not be liable (see above).

As a civil claim the burden of proof is 'on the balance of probabilities'. So, in respect of causation the test is whether, on the balance of probabilities, the tree the primary cause of the subsidence damage.

Assessing causation can require a variety of site investigation evidence and expert assessment. During the course of the site investigations evidence such as geotechnical evidence, root identification, foundation evidence and monitoring evidence are taken. When that gets to the stage of a legal claim it is common for there to be both an expert engineer and an expert arboriculturalist giving evidence to the Court, opining on the site investigation results.

But the cause of the damage is not always clear-cut. It is often not just one causal factor operating in isolation. There can be numerous causal factors all working together. So, where there is more than one thing at play, how can causation be assessed?

The case of *Solloway v Hampshire CC*[8] dealt with a claim where the property was found to be more vulnerable to tree root subsidence damage due to the shallowness of the foundations. The tree concerned was a large Poplar tree owned by Hampshire County Council. In 1976 crack damage was noticed to the property with experts agreeing that the roots of the Poplar tree were extracting moisture from the clay soil underneath the foundations. However, the house was particularly fragile and prone to movement due to the shallow foundations. The Council argued that the primary cause of the damage was the inadequate foundations and that they should not be held liable. The Court of Appeal rejected the Council's defence and held that the tree roots were the 'material cause' of the subsidence. The fact that the house was fragile did not prevent the Council from being liable. This established the eggshell skull rule within tree root subsidence cases, i.e., the Defendant must take the property as they find it.

The Court of Appeal case of *Loftus-Brigham & Anor v London Borough of Ealing*[9]_addressed the issue of causation, setting out it was not necessary for the tree roots to be the sole cause of the damage. What mattered was that they were the 'effective and substantial cause' of the subsidence. This is an expression regularly cited as a key causation principle.

Once a liability arises from the tree being found to be the material cause, damages are recoverable for the whole of the loss attributable to the nuisance, provided that the tree was one of the primary causes.

If, as is common, there are multiple trees and multiple tree owners involved, the Court can apportion damage between the relevant trees. Whilst Solloway is a leading Court of Appeal decision, the more recent

---

8 Solloway v Hampshire CC[8] [1981] 79 LGR 449

9 Loftus-Brigham & Anor v London Borough of Ealing [2003] EWCA Civ 1490

County Court decision of *Ridge v Westminster City Council*[10] dealt with the issue of apportionment.

In *Ridge* the house had suffered crack damage caused by tree root subsidence. There were several mature trees implicated in the damage owned by different third parties, including Westminster City Council. The claimant alleged that all of the tree were contributing to the damage. This raised the issue of how to deal with the question of liability where more than one defendant was potentially liable and how should damages be divided. At the London County Court the Judge accepted the expert opinion that more than one tree was a material cause of the subsidence. A liability in nuisance was found against the relevant tree owners as they had a duty to abate the nuisance once put on notice. The damages were then apportioned between the defendants to reflect the extent of the contribution of their respective trees, as set out in the engineering and arboricultural evidence.

6. Reasonable repair

When liability has been found and the quantum of the claim is being determined, the amount of damages recoverable from the defendant is another question for expert opinion.

Stabilising a property and the consequential repair works can vary in nature and scope. Just because the claimant has spent that amount of money in stabilising and repairing their property does not mean that is the amount which can be claimed back from the defendant. It is all a question of 'reasonable cost'. At this point the Court will be guided by the expert engineering opinion on whether the work carried out was both justified and reasonable in its extent and cost.

---

10 Ridge v Westminster City Council [2005] EWCA Civ 151

An example of this is the Court of Appeal case of ***Robbins v London Borough of Bexley***[11] where the Court looked at the engineering evidence and considered whether underpinning works carried out by the claimant were reasonable. The Court concluded, on the basis of the expert evidence, that the underpinning was justified given the ongoing risk to the property. This highlighted that the reasonableness of the repair works is judged against the evidence available at the time and not to be retrospectively assessed with hindsight.

7. Limitation

The starting point when considering limitation in a tree root subsidence case is found in section 2 of the Limitation Act 1980. That is that an action founded on tort must be brought within 6 years of the date when the cause of action accrued.

However, as we have set out earlier in this chapter when discussing the case of *Delaware Mansions*, pinpointing the onset of damage being caused by the action of roots underground can be difficult.

What this means is as follows.

In *Delaware Mansions* the House of Lords found that Westminster Council only became liable for the damage once they knew, or ought reasonably to have known, that their tree was causing the damage. That is the point at which the 6-year limitation period started to run.

However, in terms of abating the nuisance and the underpinning works which were carried out in the absence of tree removal, the House of Lords set out that nuisance is a continuing tort.

Lord Cooke set out:

[11] Robbins v London Borough of Bexley [2013] EWCA Civ 1619

> *"The damage was continuing, and so was the nuisance. It is settled law that a continuing nuisance gives rise to a fresh cause of action so long as it continues....In a case of continuing nuisance... the relevant time for limitation purposes is not when the damage first began to occur, but when the nuisance is continuing and not causing damage which is too remote".*

So, limitation runs from the point of notice and continuing damage, not necessarily from the date when the damage was first noticed by the claimant.

An example here could be that a homeowner noticed cracking in 2022 and investigations were carried out and concluded in early 2023. On conclusion of those investigations the Council tree owners was put on notice of the damage in spring 2023. This could be said to be when the 6-year limitation period starts to run in this claim. If the Council go on to be asked to abate the nuisance with tree removal and fail to do that and underpinning works go ahead. The second part of the Delaware test indicates that the 6-year limitation period in respect of that abatement work will run from the date that works is concluded. This can lead to different parts of the same claim having different limitation periods. In this example the investigation and superstructure work claim might run from spring 2023 whereas the underpinning part of the claim will run for 6 years from the date when that underpinning work concludes.

In practice, where there are 2 different limitation periods in the same claim, it is of course advisable to adhere to the earlier of the two.

CHAPTER THREE

MITIGATION

A claimant in a tree root subsidence claim has a duty to mitigate their loss. What this means is that, once damage is noticed and evidence shows it is a result of the action/inaction of a defendant, the claimant must act. The claimant cannot do nothing and allow matters to become worse and then expect full compensation for the worsened damage from the defendant. The claimant has a duty to mitigate their loss.

This is set out in the case of *Payzu Ltd v Saunders*[12] where Warrington LJ set out:

> *"The plaintiff is bound to take all reasonable steps to mitigate the loss consequent on the defendant's wrong, and cannot recover damages for any loss which he ought reasonably to have avoided".*

This mitigation step is key in a tree root subsidence legal claim. That is because, not only is it the overarching duty already set out, but it can affect the recoverability of damages and the scope of liability if it is not correctly exercised by the claimant.

There are mitigation expectations for both claimant and defendant in a tree root subsidence case.

1. The legal duty to mitigate by the Claimant

In the context of a tree root subsidence case, the steps the claimant must take in mitigation may involve:

---

[12] Payzu Ltd v Saunders [1919] 2 KB 581

- Telling the owner of the implicated tree of the suspected encroachment of the tree roots under the foundations of their property and and the consequent damage.
- Obtaining reasonable evidence to link the movement of the property to the tree.
- Allowing the defendant access to carry out an independent inspection of the damage if they should wish.
- Promptly removing any causes which are in the claimant's control and carrying out works which affect the structural stability of the property.

The Court will not allow the recovery of damages relating to losses which could have been avoided by the claimant. This will affect the level of recoverable damages, even where liability might otherwise be established by the claimant.

2. The duty of the Defendant

Once the Defendant is put on notice of the damage by the claimant, they are under a duty to take reasonable steps to both investigate the allegations and, where reasonable and appropriate, mitigate the ongoing risk.

Whilst the duty to mitigate is the claimant's, the defendant can review the mitigation request and raise the following points:

a) Delay

The defendant could raise that the claimant failed to act reasonably in noticing the damage and notifying the defendant of that damage, with supporting evidence, within a reasonable period of time. For example, take a claim where there is damage to an end of terrace property. Delays in the investigation work lead to the defendant council being approached with the evidence and a request to abate the nuisance a year after damage was first noticed. That intervening year is an 'event' summer and damage escalates rapidly. So much so that the flank wall now requires structural work and removal of the tree is no longer able to stop ongoing damage. Had the defendant been approached with evidence the year the damage was noticed tree work could have prevented this escalation of the damage. The defendant can argue they are not responsible for the cost of the repair work caused by the delay, even where all other elements of the claim are satisfied.

b) Failure to provide reasonable access

Where the claimant refuses reasonable attempts at investigation by the defendant, the defendant may argue that it was not given a reasonable opportunity to abate the nuisance. The defendant should be given reasonable access to the property, to site investigations, and to carry out their own investigations in order to be able to reach their own conclusion on causation and whether there is a nuisance for them to abate.

c) Unreasonable repair works

A claimant who proceeds with underpinning (or other substructure works) without first giving the defendant the chance to abate the nuisance, will be said to have acted unreasonably. The case of *Delaware Mansions* (discussed below) deals with that requirement in detail. Reasonable notice must be given.

d) Remedial works would have been ineffective

The defendant may argue that mitigation was not reasonably possible. For example, by the time they received the notice to abate, the damage was such that underpinning or other substructure work could no longer be avoided by tree removal work only. This defence will require reliance on expert arboricultural and engineering evidence.

3. <u>Delaware Mansions</u>

The House of Lords case of Delaware Mansions again comes into play in relation to mitigation and the opportunity to abate.

The Court held that liability arises once the defendant knows, or ought to know, of the damage and then fails to take reasonable steps to abate that nuisance. Both Lords Cooke and Millett set out in their judgments that the defendant must be given a reasonable opportunity to abate the nuisance once they are on notice. Only after that reasonable opportunity passes can liability crystalise.

Practically speaking this means, to comply with the requirements to give the defendant the opportunity to abate, a notice letter with evidence in support needs to be sent to the defendant tree owner to put them on notice and to make the request. The onus is then on the defendant to review the evidence and carry out reasonable work proportionate to the risk. If the defendant fails to do that and damage continues they can be liable for the cost of the reasonable remedial work.

As Lord Cooke set out:

> *"The Council cannot be held liable for damage of which they had no knowledge, actual or constructive. But once they were told of the continuing damage being caused by the tree, they were under a duty to take reasonable steps within a reasonable*

> *time to abate the nuisance. They had to be given the opportunity to do so. If, after that opportunity, they failed to act, they became liable for the consequences"*

The point on opportunity to abate and mitigation was considered by the Court of Appeal in the later case of *L.E.Jones (Insurance Brokers) Ltd v Portsmouth City Council [2002]*.[13]

In the LE Jones case the defendant tree owner had not been given the opportunity to abate the nuisance before the underpinning work went ahead. The claimant sought to recover those underpinning costs despite that. The Court of Appeal held that, because the Council tree owner had not been given a reasonable opportunity to deal with the problem, the cost of the underpinning could not be recovered in full. However, some underpinning costs were awarded to the claimant despite this failure. That was because the Court of Appeal allowed the claimant to recover the reasonable proportion of costs that reflected what would have been incurred anyway had the council been given a chance and then the Council had acted reasonably in response.

The claimant tried to argue that the failure to write to the defendant was due to the fact that they knew from past experience that the defendant would take no action in response to an opportunity to abate letter. However, the Court of Appeal reiterated that the law required the claimant to give the defendant the opportunity to abate and that the step could not be skipped on the presumption that the Defendant would ignore or refuse to abate the nuisance. If the step is skipped that is a failure to mitigate.

13 L.E.Jones (Insurance Brokers) Ltd v Portsmouth City Council [2002] EWCA Civ 1723

4. How long is reasonable?

It is often asked what a reasonable period of time is for a claimant to give a defendant to abate a nuisance. There is not a one-size-fits-all answer to this and the Court have not set out what a reasonable period of time is.

The element of reasonableness will mean this depends on the level of evidence given to the defendant, how serious the damage is, the urgency of repair works, the time of year that the request is made and the resources of the defendant.

Claimants can work around a 3 to 6-month time frame as being a starting point for a reasonable period of time but both claimants and defendants should be alive to the facts of each situation and where this period of time might be either generous or, conversely, unreasonably short.

5. Duty to Consult (England)

The Environment Act 2021 introduced the duty to consult on street tree felling. This duty was a government response to the number of high-profile street tree felling programs by some local authorities in England which had been incredibly unpopular with local residents. An example of one such situation was the Sheffield Street Tree situation which resulted in the Independent Inquiry into the Street Trees Dispute in Sheffield, chaired by Sir Mark Lowcock (2022).

This new duty is found in section 115 and Schedule 16 of the Act. It means that highway authorities in England now have a legal duty to consult with the public before felling certain street trees.

The duty applies where a local highway authority proposes to fell an urban street tree so will not apply to all cases involving Council owned trees.

The consultation duty is that the local authority must consult local residents and other relevant stakeholders about the tree work proposal. This usually means posting the proposal online and displaying a notice on the tree or in its immediate vicinity so that local residents are aware of it. The notice has to stay up for at least 28 days, which is considered to be the minimum consultation period.

Following the consultation period the guidance sets out that the Local Highways Authority should give consideration and weight to the representations made and make the outcome of the consultation public for a period of 2 years.

As with other sorts of tree application, there are exemptions to the requirement to carry out a consultation. For example, if the tree is dead, dangerous, diseased or poses an urgent safety risk. The onus is on the Highway Authority to ensure that there is sufficient evidence to prove that a street tree is exempt from the duty to consult as non-compliance could lead to legal challenge.

If complaints arise around how the duty of consult has been exercised, the route is to complain via the Local Authority's complaint process and then on to the Local Government & Social Care Ombudsman if the complaints process did not resolve matters. There is also the option of a Judicial Review. However Judicial Review proceedings must be started within 6 weeks of the outcome of the consultation so would need to be started before the complaints process is concluded otherwise the timeframe would be missed.

6. Joint mitigation protocol

Given the number of tree root subsidence claims and the time and evidence intense nature of the investigations, the industry has worked to create an agreed protocol to manage the mitigation stage of a tree root subsidence claim involving a local authority owned tree.

The first Joint Mitigation Protocol (JMP) was launched by the London Tree Officer's Association in the early 2000s. The aim being to try and avoid these tree root subsidence cases becoming entrenched legal disputes. That was updated in 2008 and is undergoing a further update at the moment.

The JMP is in consultation phase with the industry and should be launched in late 2025.

The purpose of this protocol is to create a voluntary process agreed with both home insurers and local authorities to allow for the management of tree root subsidence claims aligning with fair levels of evidence and running in tandem with the duty to consult.

Whilst the JMP will be a voluntary protocol and adherence to it, or not, will not be a technical point to raise in any tree root subsidence litigation, it has political support and is likely to be taken into account in future legal cases when the Court are asked to consider the reasonableness of behavior of both parties.

There is a risk to both parties that failure to engage in an industry accepted protocol, leading to a more protracted situation and an increase in both repair and litigation costs, could lead to the Court limiting damages and/or imposing costs sanctions in later litigation.

7. Can pruning successfully mitigate?

A practical question often raised is whether tree pruning can be sufficient to abate a nuisance, or whether only removal of the tree will do.

Pruning and pollarding of trees reduce the crown volume, thereby reducing transpiration. In theory, this can lessen water demand and mitigate subsidence. However, how effective pruning is as a method to manage nuisance is a point of debate as the effect of pruning can be variable.

Engineering consensus (see *Hortlink*[14] research programmes) is that pruning can stabilise ground and property in some cases, but reliability is low, and the pruning needs to be maintained on a regular cycle, requiring ongoing commitment by the tree owner.

Legal Implications

As we have said above, the duty on the tree owner is to take reasonable steps once damage is foreseeable but what counts as "reasonable" depends on the situation.

- If expert advice suggests cyclical crown reduction is likely to control the problem, then pruning might be a reasonable response.
- If, however, evidence shows pruning is ineffective or that movement continues despite repeated reductions, then the only "reasonable" step may be tree removal.
- Courts have been reluctant to impose draconian regimes where the outcome is uncertain and the tree's amenity is severely compromised (*Pattichis v Enfield* illustrates this).

[14] Hotlink 212 (East Malling Research and University of Cambridge. Controlling water use of trees to alleviate subsidence risk (Horticulture LINK Project 212). and Beyond Hortlink 212 (Hipps NA and Atkinson CJ. Pilot study to determine the feasibility of using existing data to determine the impacts of tree pruning on subsidence incidents on swelling clay soils)

The Risk of Continuing Liability

Where pruning is attempted but fails to stop ongoing damage, the tree owner can remain legally liable.

Insurers' Perspective

Insurers can often be seen to require felling rather than cyclical pruning to provide their insured with a definite conclusion to the insurance claim. Monitoring of the property will typically follows any reduction works to check that the property stabilises following that tree work. If movement of the property continues, pressure can be on to get the tree felled. The Financial Ombudsman Service has taken the view that insurers must fund a lasting repair, not a temporary measure (see Chapter 10).

CHAPTER FOUR

LEGAL REMEDIES

Where there is a liability in negligence or nuisance for damage caused by tree root subsidence the claimant has a number of legal remedies available to them. These can include damages, injunctions, abatement and declarations.

Negligence

In negligence the main remedy is damages with the aim of damages being to put the claimant back into the position that they would have been in 'but for' the negligence. The remedy is focused on compensation with heads of damages including the cost of repair works, alternative accommodation and consequential losses.

In negligence recovery of damages for 'pure economic loss', i.e., a loss which is not as a result of physical damage to a property, is not permitted. Most tree root subsidence claims clearly involve damage to property however, where there are arguments about the diminution in value of land or property where no damage has occurred, this could lead to arguments about pure economic loss as a bar to the recovery of that claimed loss.

Nuisance

There are a wider variety of remedies available in a claim of private nuisance. Those include injunctions to stop or limit the nuisance; damages to recover compensation for the loss; abatement action and declaratory relief.

1. Damages

Damages are the most common remedy sought in tree root subsidence cases and are there to compensate for the damage caused to the property by the tree. Damages sought in a tree root subsidence claim can be split into general and special damages.

General Damages

General damages are losses which flow from the 'wrong' and can be assessed by the Court, such as loss of amenity and inconvenience. There is no standard amount of general damages awarded in a tree root subsidence claim. Past court decisions point to the amount of money that the Court is likely to award under this heading being very modest. For example:

- *Eiles v Southwark London Borough Council [2006]*[15] in which the Court awarded £1,500 in general damages to reflect the disturbance and inconvenience to the Claimant.
- *Robbins v Bexley LBC [2013]*[16] – where the Court awarded £1,500 – £2,000
- *Pattichis v Enfield [2016] –* £2,000

So general damages are awarded usually in the £1,500-£2,000 range regardless of the extent of the damage and the duration of the ongoing damage to the property.

---

15 Eiles v Southwark London Borough Council [2006] EWHC 1411

16 Robbins v London Borough of Bexley [2013] EWHC 2253 (QB)

Special damages

Special damages are the particular financial losses which flow from the wrong and which can be quantified and evidenced. These include items such as:

a. Repair costs

The claimant is entitled to recover the cost of a reasonable repair scheme in relation to the subsidence damage, this could include demolition and rebuild, underpinning, crack stitching and other innovative repair solutions coming onto the market. When making a claim to recover this cost it should be supported by expert comment on the nature, scope and reasonableness of the repair scheme. The Court will look at that evidence and scrutinse whether the works were necessary and proportionate.

b. Investigation costs

Costs incurred to investigate the damage and to establish liability and causation will generally be recovered. As discussed earlier, this can include geotechnical investigations, root analysis, arboricultural assessment and monitoring of the property. Again, the recoverability is limited to what was reasonably incurred.

c. Consequential losses

Repair work in tree root subsidence cases can often require the homeowners moving out of the property whilst the repair works go ahead. This can particularly be so where damage is focused on areas of the property such as the kitchen and bathroom areas, meaning that living in the property is no longer feasible. Again, reasonableness is key here and alternative accommodation will have to have been reasonably necessary and reasonable in its duration and nature. Further, such losses can include storage costs (if contents need to be removed), any business interruption costs (in commercial cases) and professional fees incurred in the investigation of the claim. These are distinct from the professional fees of experts involved later on in the litigation.

d. Mitigation losses

Where it has not been possible to stop ongoing seasonal movement caused by the tree, by removal of the tree, other mitigation losses such as underpinning, installation of a tree root barrier or resin injection can be recovered. Mitigation is judged at the time the decision is made to carry out this work and it must be supported by expert evidence as being a reasonable and proportionate solution.

2. Injunctions

An injunction is an order sought from the Court either compelling or prohibiting someone from doing something. An injunction to force action is a mandatory injunction and an injunction to stop something is a prohibitory injunction.

An injunction is an equitable remedy so it is routed in discretion and fairness. It can be awarded by the Court where it is felt that damages would not be sufficient.

In tree root subsidence claims an injunction can be sought to compel the defendant tree owner to carry out work to their tree. However, injunctions are discretionary and in these cases, where insurance cover is in place and an alternative stabilisation solution such as underpinning is available, the Court is prone to object to granting an injunction.

The case of *Lemmon v Webb [1894]*[17] is a Court of Appeal case dealing with overhanging branches. In that case the Court refused the injunction as the claimant had the self-help remedy of cutting overhanging branches therefore abating the nuisance themselves

3. Abatement

The right of abatement as a self-help remedy in the law of nuisance. This has already been covered off in the Mitigation chapter (chapter 3).

This is the claimant's common law right to take steps to prevent, reduce or stop a nuisance without the need for a Court order. In tree root subsidence cases this can involve pruning roots and branches back to a boundary line and installing tree root barriers to prevent further root encroachment.

In order to exercise a right of abatement there are a few conditions:

1. The claimant must exercise this right from their own land as entering onto a neighbour's land without permission could be trespass.

2. The work must be reasonable and proportionate, for example the claimant cannot carry out work to a neighbour's tree from their side of the boundary if to that work could negatively affect the health of the tree.

3. Any items removed, e.g., branches, roots or fallen fruit, still belongs to the tree owner and should be returned to them or be offered back to them.

In tree root subsidence the abatement of the nuisance can be more difficult as it can risk damaging or destabilising the tree and also it is

[17] Lemmon v Webb [1894] 3 Ch 1

not a permanent solution to the subsidence problem which will just return if the tree is left to regrow.

4. Declaratory Relief

This is a tool which can be used to facilitate an outcome for parties involved in a dispute. It is where the Court is asked to make a formal declaration on a legal position between the parties. It is something that can give clarity to a position. For example it could be used to determine issues concerning a boundary and also to determine whether a tree is causing a legal nuisance.

Whilst this is not a UK case, the case of *Bonde v Bishop.*[18] This was a case in the California Court of Appeal which dealt with an application for declaratory relief where the Court was asked to formally declare that the defendant's tree, overhanging the claimant's property, constituted a nuisance. The Court responded by declaring that it was a nuisance and ordering abatement of the nuisance and nominal damages.

5. Court applications

Whilst Court applications are not a remedy in themselves, they can be a process by which a remedy is sought and obtained. Part 8 of the Civil Procedure Rules is a way in which a Court application can be made.

For example, where access is needed to a neighbour's land in order to be able to carry out repair works to the claimant's property, an application can be made under the Access to Neighbouring Land Act 1992 where access is not granted voluntarily. Such an order by the Court gives the applicant temporary rights to go onto a neighbour's land to carry out basic preservation works to their own property.

[18] Bonde v Bishop Civ. No. 15163. First Dist., Div. One. June 25, 1952

Whilst not a remedy in itself, such an application can bring about the conclusion of the repair works to a property.

6. Mediation

Mediation is not a remedy in the truest sense of the word but this book should not be written without comment on mediation as an important process in reaching solutions in these legal claims. Mediation is a way of resolving a dispute without going through litigation. It is a voluntary and confidential process where the parties resolve a dispute with the help and assistance of the facilitating mediator. Attending a mediation is cheaper and quicker than litigation and can allow disputes to be concluded whilst keeping stress levels lower and preserving relationships between the parties. When litigating the Courts encourage parties to mediate and this is moving more towards compulsory mediation as is now the case in the small claims track.

CHAPTER FIVE

THE LAW OF SUBROGATION

A legal claim in nuisance to recover damages following tree root subsidence is a claim brought by the homeowner claimant from the tree owner defendant. However, the legal claims themselves are brought by the insurer of the claimant, but are pursued using the name of their insured. This is due to the equitable principle of subrogation.

Subrogation means the substitution of one person for another. *MacGillivray on Insurance Law*[19] sets out that

> *'In insurance law "subrogation" is the name given to the right of the insurer who has paid a loss to be put in the place of the assured so that he can take advantage of any means available to the assured to extinguish or diminish the loss for which the insurer has indemnified the assured.'.*

MacGillivray goes on to set out that the doctrine confers two distinct rights on the insurer after payment of a loss.

1. The first is to receive the benefit of all rights and remedies of the insured against third parties which, if satisfied, will extinguish or diminish the ultimate loss sustained.

2. The second is to claim from their insured any benefit conferred on the insured by third parties with the aim of compensating

[19] MacGillivray on Insurance Law, Sweet & Maxwell

the insured for the loss in respect of which the insurers has indemnified them.

What does this mean in tree root subsidence cases?

Most domestic property damage caused by tree root subsidence will be covered, at least in part, by household buildings insurance. Once the insurance claim has been accepted by insurers under the policy of insurance, the insurance company will manage the claim, deal with mitigation and repair the property. On conclusion of the repair works the insurer can then step into the shoes of their insured to pursue the legal recovery claim, i.e., to pursue the claim in nuisance against the tree owner. This is done in the name of their insured although, to all intents and purposes, it is the insurer that is funding and managing the legal claim.

As part of the one legal claim there will be both insured losses and uninsured losses.

Insured losses

Insured losses are any financial loss not only paid in the insurance claim but contractually falling within the scope of the policy indemnity. In tree root subsidence claims these losses can include:

- Site investigation work
- Drain survey
- Engineering and arboricultrual reports
- Monitoring and level surveys
- Repair works, both substructure and superstructure

- Alternative accommodation and storage costs

When a tree root subsidence claim is made, the insurers will most likely outsource the claim to be managed by one of their external suppliers. These loss adjusting companies incur fees for the management of the claim which insurers pay. The recovery of loss adjusting fees, whilst an insured loss, are largely irrecoverable in a legal recovery claim.

In the claim of *Cuthbert v Gair & Gair (2008)*[20] the High Court addressed the issue of the recoverability of loss adjusters' fees in a personal injury claim. In that case the Court noted that under subrogation the insurer steps into the insured's shoes, but the insured is not liable for adjusters' fees so there can be no loss for the insurer to subrogate. Therefore, adjuster fees do not count as recoverable damages in tree root subsidence litigation.

Uninsured losses

As well as the insured losses incurred by the insurance company, their insured will also likely incur financial losses which are not reimbursed by their insurer. An example of such an uninsured loss is the insurance policy excess. There could be other uninsured losses such as losses reasonably linked to the tree root subsidence but not covered by the policy wording. Loss exceeding the policy limits could result in uninsured losses stemming from under insurance for example.

The general damages referred to in Chapter 4 will fall within this heading of uninsured losses.

[20] Cuthbert v Gair [1968] 1 WLR 1310 (QBD)

Settlement & conflict

Where both the insured and uninsured losses stem from the same insurance claim, they must be pursued together as one legal claim. It is common for the insurance company's general terms and conditions of the insurance policy to set out that they will manage the legal claim and will include the recovery of uninsured losses on behalf of their insured.

The House of Lords case of *Napier & Ettrick v Hunter [1993]*[21] addresses the issue of the apportionment of damages between insured and uninsured losses. In that case it sets out that, if there is a recovery where the amount of damages covers both insured and uninsured losses, the recovery should be applied in a structured order:

1. Insured being entitled to their uninsured losses first

2. Only after that can the insurer recoup what has been paid out under the policy

Solicitors pursuing recovery claims in tree root subsidence to ensure that they have authority from both the insurer and the insured when reaching a settlement in a claim as the damages can belong to both.

One bite of the cherry

The general terms and conditions of an insurance policy will give the insurer the contractual right to manage the legal recovery claim and ensure that the insured does not prejudice the insurers rights in a legal claim. Often the insured may not be aware of this policy term and might well have gone ahead to issue legal proceedings themselves to recover their uninsured losses from the tree owner. If that happens without the insurer being aware before the claim concludes, it might

[21] Napier & Ettrick v Hunter [1993] AC 713

lead to a breach of contract claim between the insurer and their insured. If this happens and the insurer becomes aware of the situation before the claim concludes, it is likely to lead to the prompt amendment of the legal claim to add the insured losses into the claim and for the management of that claim to be taken over by the insurance company's legal representative.

Both the insured losses and uninsured losses from a tree root subsidence claim are one claim. If those losses are settled by either the insurance company or their insured to the exclusion of the other, it needs to be made clear in the compromise agreement with the third party the limit of the settlement. For example, the insured settling the claim without prejudice to the recovery of the insured losses.

Does it apply in the Lands Chamber?

Where a tree root subsidence claim leads to a claim for compensation pursuant to s202E of the Town and Country Planning Act (see Chapter 9) the law of subrogation does not apply. These claims belong to the landowner and so are pursued in the name of the insured as the property owner. Careful agreement between the insurer and insured needs to be reached to ensure that any compensation received in this claim is returned to the insurer rather than retained by their insured.

Where such a claim is pursued in the name of the insurance company, rather than the landowner, it is assumed that there has been a contractual assignment to the benefit of the claim to the insurer by their insured.

CHAPTER SIX

DIFFERENT TREE OWNERS

A tree root subsidence claim can vary depending on the type of tree owner. Trees can be owned by domestic homeowners, local authorities, landlords, commercial landowners, developers, housing associations and government agencies, to name a few.

This chapter picks out some common third parties who appear in subsidence claims and reviews how claims again them can differ.

1. Domestic property owners

Domestic property owners owe a duty of care to their neighbours not to let trees in their ownership cause foreseeable damage. That means that if they knew, or ought reasonably to have known, that roots from their trees were encroaching onto the claimant's land and could cause damage then they might be legally liable for that damage.

On the issue of foreseeability there are two points which arise. The first is whether the risk of subsidence damage caused by the tree to the property was something which a reasonable lay person could have foreseen. The case of *Khan & Khan v Harrow Council & Kane [2013]* the Court viewed the Cypress tree and held the neighbour to be liable as it was foreseeable to any reasonable tree owner that the tree could cause damage due to its size and proximity to the property.

The second point relates to the ABI Domestic Subsidence Tree Root Claims Agreement, Third Party Liability. This is an agreement between household insurance companies where each subscribing insurer agrees to the following. The insurer of the claimant property will not pursue a recovery against the insurer of the domestic defendant property responsible for the tree root encroachment regardless of whether the damage to the claimant property has been caused wholly or partly by the tree root encroachment. However, in the event of there being a recurrence of the damage or no reasonable preventive measures taken with the person having liability for the tree root encroachment, the agreement will have no effect in relation to a subsequent claim. This agreement mirrors elements of foreseeability.

Where a domestic property owner receives correspondence from the insurer of the damaged property, that will first be an approach with a request to mitigate. At this stage of the 'claim' the tree owner might notify their own insurer about this approach but their insurer will not necessarily get involved in the claim at that stage. At the point at which an approach is in relation to a claim in nuisance, the tree owner should notify their insurer who may provide them with an indemnity in respect of any liability.

2. Local Authorities

Local authorities can be involved in tree root subsidence claims in various capacities. For the purpose of this section we are considering whether the local authority themselves are the tree owner.

Local authorities are subject to the same legal duty in negligence and nuisance as a private landowner. However, in tree root subsidence cases it can be observed that the Court can impose a higher standard of care due to their technical knowledge and the size of their tree stock.

Unlike private owners, local authorities are expected to have systems in place for inspection and risk management, with arboricultural officers or contractors monitoring trees. The higher bar in terms of their knowledge may mean that they are less able to claim ignorance where damage occurs. However other factors raise issues around the reasonableness of their tree maintenance regimes and whether those can be relied on to defend allegations of falling short of their duty of care in management.

Pressures facing local authorities include resource pressures, budget limits and policy constraints. Trees are being managed by different departments within one local authority, for example the highways department, planning department and the tree department. Trees are being inspected for safety, disease and amenity purposes as well as for the risk of damage from events such as tree root subsidence.

Where claims are made against a local authority tree owner they will have insurance cover in respect of a liability. Often those insurance policies have large deductibles so that if a legal claim is of modest value and falls under the deductible amount it can be addressed by the local authority without referring to insurers.

With the duty to consult affecting local authorities who wish to remove a street tree implicated in subsidence damage, the landscape for these tree owners is changing. There is political support from Government for the Joint Mitigation Protocol in the hope that a consensus between the insurers of domestic properties damaged by subsidence and local authority tree owners can be reached to reduce friction and speed up the handling of these claims for all concerned.

3. Commercial third parties

For commercial landowners such as Network Rail, utility providers, developers or other large landowners, claims against them can be nuanced. They still have duties under nuisance and negligence but the Court can have different expectations.

For the likes of infrastructure providers who might, for example, own a significant number of trees along a railway network, the Courts expect a level of systemisation in inspection and maintenance, much like with local authorities. Claims against these types of commercial third party can often focus on evidence around whether a reasonable inspection regime was in place and whether signs of risk were ignored or missed.

Due to the resources that a commercial third party have they often defend claims robustly on causation and can also bring in points regarding wider public and safety issues in their defences.

Repair works to damaged properties adjacent to land owned by one of these owners can be difficult. For example, repairing properties adjacent to land being managed by an infrastructure provider can be difficult for numerous reasons, most notably safety. This can require a complex, expensive and protracted set of applications and approvals before access is granted to safely carry out repairs.

See *Hilda's Montessori Nursery Ltd v Tesco Stores Ltd [2006]*[22] as an example of a claim against a corporate tree owner.

4. Housing Associations and Institutional Landowners

These entities often manage large estates with communal gardens and open spaces and a significant tree stock. They too will be expected to maintain a reasonable system of inspection of their trees. Whilst a Court will judge them against the standard of a reasonable landowner that will reflect their organisational knowledge and capacity. Liability may arise if they fail to respond to complaints, ignore evidence from surveys or allow obvious risks to continue across their estate. Often claims can be slow due to work being outsourced and spread across various departments. Whilst insurance cover will be in place, claims can be slow to progress due to the 'red tape' of stakeholders involved and the outsourcing of services.

---

[22] Hilda's Montessori Nursery Ltd v Tesco Stores Ltd [2006][22] EWHC 1487 (TCC), [2006] All ER (D) 313 (Jun)

5. Government or Crown Bodies

Claims involving trees on land owned by government departments can follow slightly different procedural rules. Whilst underlying duties in nuisance and negligence are the same, the procedure is different in that civil claims against the Crown are governed by the Crown Proceedings Act 1947. No claim can be brought against "the Crown", the particular department needs to be identified. These institutions usually have inspection systems and dedicated estate teams but pre-action correspondence can involve long internal reviews and involvement of government legal advisers. Claimants may face arguments about public interest or operational necessity, particularly on sensitive land.

6. Bona vacantia land

Where land is bona vacantia or the owner cannot be traced, claimants face difficulty in identifying a defendant. Bona vacantia land technically falls to the Crown, but the Crown generally holds it passively and resists liability unless it has taken active control. In cases of dissolved companies, unregistered parcels, or unclear boundaries, claimants may need to pursue Land Registry investigations or court directions, but often the practical route is limited to abatement rather than damages, as there may be no viable party to pursue.

CHAPTER SEVEN

WHAT COURT AND WHAT PROTOCOL?

Tree root subsidence claims are civil litigation claims stemming from property damage. Whilst parties are encouraged to settle disputes without the need for litigation, there are times when disputes do require litigation and determination at Court.

County Court and High Court

These claims in nuisance and negligence are civil claims falling within the jurisdiction of the County Court or the High Court, depending on value and complexity. The majority of cases are issued in the County Court and include claims for damages to compensate for damage to a domestic property, other insured losses and the modest amount of general damages. If the claim is under £100,000 in value and does not include a particularly complex or novel point, it will generally remain in the County Court.

Once issued the claim will be allocated to a track under Part 26 of the Civil Procedure Rules. Generally speaking:

- Small claims track – claims under £10,000

- Fast track – claims between £10,000 and £25,000.

- Intermediate track – claims between £25,000 and £100,000. The intermediate track being split into four complexity bands

- Multi track – Typically claims over £100,000.

Claims are suitable for the High Court where the claim value exceeds £100,000 and where there are complex issues of law, expert evidence of issues of public interest. When issuing in the High Court these claims are run in the Kings Bench Division, possibly in one of the specialist lists such as the Technology and Construction Court, but otherwise within the general KBD list. Whilst claims of significant value and importance can be issued at the Royal Courts of Justice in London, use can be made of the High Court District Registries across the UK such as Manchester, Cardiff, Birmingham and Leeds.

Pre-Action Protocol

This is no particular pre action protocol which relates to tree root subsidence claims. Generally, solicitors treat tree root subsidence cases as falling under the principles of the Practice Direction on Pre Action Conduct, and this will be referenced in the letter of claim. If there are other elements to the claim, such as professional negligence, one of the other Pre Action Protocols might become appropriate.

Upper Tribunal, Lands Chamber

As set out in Chapter 9, claims for compensation against a planning authority following a Notice of Refusal being issued in relation to a TPO application, are brought before the Upper Tribunal of the Lands Chamber.

The Tribunal Procedure (Upper Tribunal) (Lands Chamber) Rules 2010 apply in these cases.

CHAPTER EIGHT

COMMON DEFENCES

Having considered how to bring a claim, this chapter considers common defences which are raised in tree root subsidence claims.

1. We are not responsible for the tree

Ownership of a tree and responsibility for its maintenance is often unclear. The following cases are ones in which the defence of 'we do not owe a duty of care' was raised.

In *Solloway v Hampshire County Council [1981]*[23] the issue raised was whether the trees which were alleged to have caused damage to the claimant's property by trees growing on land associated with a school. The question was whether Hampshire County Council (the education authority and landowner) or the District Council (who carried out maintenance) were responsible. The Court of Appeal found that Hampshire County Council remained liable because it was the landowner with ultimate control of the trees even though another authority handled the day-to-day maintenance.

In the case of *Russell v London Borough of Barnet* Barnet argued in their defence that they did not owe a duty of care as the trees were not owned by them. They argued that they were owned by the property owners adjoining the highway where the trees were located as those owners were deemed to be the owners of the subsoil. Since the trees were growing from that subsoil Barnet argued the property owners therefore owned the trees. In that case it was found that

[23] Solloway v Hampshire County Council [1981][23] 79 LGR 449 (CA)

> *"even if it were correct and that Barnet as highway authority did not own the trees planted in the pavement or the verges where they alone have the power to maintain the trees and if damage or obstruction to the highway is caused, to cut them down, then this is sufficient control over the tree to make them liable for nuisance if such occurs."*

In *Delaware Mansions* the House of Lords addressed the issues of responsibility for the trees causing subsidence. The Court set out that Westminster could not avoid liability by pointing to contractors or saying that the damage started before Delaware became the freeholders. Westminster owned and controlled the tree and that made them the responsible party even though the tree had been there long before the claimant purchased the property and the duty was owed to them in particular.

2. The tree is protected by a TPO, we could not do anything

Where a tree protected by a TPO is the cause of subsidence damage, a tree owner could raise in their defence that they were unable to do anything to their tree as it was protected. However, regardless of the protection, TPO trees are subject to normal duties of care and the protection under a TPO does not relieve the owner of a common law liability.

3. It's not my tree

Trees can often grow on or close to boundaries and a dispute can arise on whether the tree belongs to the defendant or not. In relation to the ownership of a tree, the Court looks at where the trunk stands and who exercises control of the tree. This can often turn on the particular facts of case. Reference to land registry documents to determine a boundary line or instruction of a boundary surveyor could be required in order to help determine ownership.

4. We acted reasonably

The duty in tree root subsidence cases is one of reasonable care, it is not strict liability. *Delaware* makes it clear that the question is whether reasonable steps were taken once the risk was foreseeable.

In the case of *Berent v Family Mosaic Housing & Islington LBC* the court referred to those reasonable steps. The defendants said that the damage was not reasonable foreseeable at the relevant time. The Court held that the duty is a duty to do that which is reasonable in all the circumstances and no more than what, if anything, is responsible to prevent or minimise the known risk of damage to one's neighbour or his property. The expert evidence supported the conclusion that, while the Defendants should have known that trees could cause damage in general, predicting which trees would cause damage was not possible, and no evidence showed that the relevant tees should have been identified as a specific risk before the damage occurred. The Court found no breach of duty in failing to remove or prune the trees earlier.

5. We have not got the resources

A defendant tree owner can often be restricted by limited budgets which raises the question of whether a limit budget could be a defence to a tree root subsidence claim.

The case of *Leakey v National Trust [1980]*[24] is not a tree root subsidence case but is a nuisance case in which the defendant raised arguments about resources in their defence. In the Court of Appeal Megaw LJ said:

> *"the duty is to do that which is reasonable in all the circumstances, an no more than what is reasonable. The considerations which may be relevant are the extent of the risk,*

[24] Leakey v National Trust [1980] QB 485

the gravity of the likely damage, the practiability of preventing or minimising the known risk, and the resources available to the defendant for the purpose. It is not the duty of the defendant, whether an individual or a charitable trust, to do everything that could possibly be done; it is sufficient if he does that which is reasonable to expect of him"

6. The damage was not foreseeable

In the case of *Berent* the Court of Appeal held that the defendants were not liable because, until they had notice of actual damage, it was not reasonably foreseeable that their trees would cause the subsidence damage. It depends on foreseeability of this kind of damage. The Court commented on what is a "real risk", when a tree owner must act and what steps are reasonable in such a situation.

In response to an allegation that the property is in a 'hot spot' area for subsidence the defendant may point to a generalised risk of subsidence not being enough. There has to be a foreseeable risk from a particular tree.

Foreseeability has been considered further by the Central London County Court in the case of *Pattichis v London Borough of Enfield*. The claimants pointed to 17 previous claims in the area as evidence of this being a hot spot area for subsidence claims. However, it was held that although the property was on shrinkable clay, close to a Norway Maple and the area had a history of subsidence claims, those risk factors alone did not make damage reasonably foreseeable.

The NHBC Chapter 4.2 guidance on building near trees can be cited in relation to foreseeability. Where foundations are shallower than the recommended depth (when constructed) tree owners can argue the damage was not foreseeable as they were permitted to presume that foundations would be built to a depth recommended in industry guidance.

7. The tree owner was not 'on notice'

It is clear from Berent that the foreseeability must be in relation to the *kind* of damage. So, for example, had the local authority tree owner been approached previously about the tree and been told it was a concern for other reasons such as direct physical damage of roots or the potential for the tree to fail in a storm and cause impact damage, that would not make tree root subsidence damage caused by that same tree foreseeable.

8. The tree pre-dated the property

The defence of the tree 'being there first' is a common one to be raised by defendants and there is not one answer as to whether this defence will be successful.

In nuisance it can be said that 'coming to a nuisance' is not a defence. In other words, a claimant can still sue if their property suffers damage even if the tree pre-dated the property. That principle comes from the case of *Sturges v Bridgman (1879)*[25] in which the Court of Appeal said that what matters is whether the activity is a nuisance at the time it interferes with the claimant's reasonable use and enjoyment, not who got there first.

9. The foundations are too shallow

A common defence is that the property that has been built is too vulnerable to damage and that its construction did not take into account the presence of the trees.

The *egg shell skull rule* sets out that the defendant should 'take their victim as they find them', i.e., they just have to face the consequences

[25] Sturges v Bridgman (1879) 11 Ch D 852

of the shallow foundations making the property more vulnerable to damage. However, this rule overlaps with points on foreseeability.

Tree root subsidence damage often occurs to newer additions to a property which have been added since the original construction, for example conservatories, extensions and porches. The defendant could argue that the damage would not have been foreseeable to them as they should reasonably have been able to assume that the foundations of the newly constructed additions were designed to take into account the already-present trees. As such, damage as a result of the shallow foundations would not have been foreseeable.

10. Opportunity to abate was not given

The case of Delaware Mansions set out that the defendant should be given the opportunity to abate the nuisance before being faced with an expensive claim to recover substructure repair works. Where an opportunity to abate had not been received by the Defendant, or where the defendant was not given a reasonable period of time to exercise that opportunity to abate, this could be raised in their defence.

11. The tree was not the cause

One of the most common arguments in the defence of a tree root subsidence claim is that the evidence does not support the assertion that the tree is the primary cause of the damage to the property. As a civil claim the burden of proof for the claimant to reach is 'on the balance of probabilities'. In their defence the defendant could submit their own expert arboricultural and engineering evidence setting out an alternative conclusion that the causation evidence does not show that the tree is the primary cause.

Reference is made back to Chapter 2 in relation to contribution. The defendant could argue that, whilst their tree contributed, it was not the substantial and effective cause and therefore they have no liability. If there was a contributing cause owned by the claimant, the defendant could raise allegations of contributory negligence in their defence.

A defence on causation will be fact and evidence specific and this is where the defendant will guided by, and rely on, the opinions of their own experts.

12. The extent of the repair work is unreasonable

Delaware Mansions sets out the principle that the claimant can recover the reasonable remedial cost of abating the nuisance. As such, a defendant could seek to argue that the work carried out by the claimant was not reasonable whether that is in its scope or cost. The defendant's own expert engineer might comment on a reasonable remedial solution and the scope of the work that was carried out.

13. Minimal damage – *de minimis* argument

This argument can be raised where there may have been some movement but the defendant considers this to be too trivial to be actionable in nuisance. In nuisance cases the Court have established the maxim *de minimis non curat lex* (the law does not concern itself with trifles). What this can mean in tree root subsidence is that minor, hairline cracking which is not progressive (i.e., getting worse each year) is too minor to give rise to a liability. In this respect we refer to the BRE Guide on assessing cracks in houses.

The BRE Digest 251 sets out the following categories:

Category 0	Hairline cracks of less than about 0.1 mm which are classed as negligible. *No action required.*
Category 1	Fine cracks that *can be treated easily using normal decoration.* Damage generally restricted to internal wall finishes; cracks rarely visible in external brickwork. Typical crack widths up to 1 mm.
Category 2	*Cracks easily filled. Recurrent cracks can be masked by suitable linings.* Cracks not necessarily visible externally; some *external repointing* may be required to ensure weather-tightness. Doors and windows may stick slightly and require easing and adjusting. Typical crack widths up to 5 mm.
Category 3	*Cracks that require some opening up and can be patched by a mason. Repointing of external brickwork and possibly a small amount of brickwork to be replaced.* Doors and windows sticking. Service pipes may fracture. Weather-tightness often impaired. Typical crack widths are 5 to 15 mm, or several of, say, 3 mm.
Category 4	*Extensive damage which requires breaking-out and replacing sections of walls,* especially over doors and windows. Windows and door frames distorted, floor sloping noticeably. Walls leaning or bulging noticeably, some loss of bearing in beams. Service pipes disrupted. Typical crack widths are 15 to 25 mm, but also depends on number of cracks.

Category 5	*Structural damage that requires a major repair job, involving partial or complete rebuilding.* Beams lose bearing, walls lean badly and require shoring. Windows broken with distortion. Danger of instability. Typical crack widths are greater than 25 mm, but depends on number of cracks.

The BRE notes that, in general categories, 0, 1 and 2 can be regarded as aesthetic issues that only require redecoration. A defendant might refer to the category of damage in support of a defence of de minimis. However, note that tree root subsidence is progressive so the category of damage can change from one summer to the next if movement is left unabated.

14. Value of the tree

Local authority tree owners are increasingly concerned about the loss of trees implicated in tree root subsidence damage. The CAVAT tree valuation system allows for a financial value to put onto an amenity tree owned by a local authority. Where a tree is implicated in damage and its financial value exceeds the cost of the reasonable repair works to the property, the argument may be raised that tree removal is disproportionate. This is not an argument which has reached the Court yet but it will be interesting to see how a Court addresses such a defence when it is raised.

15. Repay CAVAT value

There is also a move towards seeking the recovery of the CAVAT value of a lost tree where a request for mitigation was made, a tree was removed and ongoing movement thereafter confirmed the removed tree was not the primary cause.

16. Limitation period missed

Limitation periods have been set out in Chapter 2. Raising limitation in the defence to a claim has the ability to prevent the claim from succeeding even if all other elements in nuisance are successful. Where limitation is being raised in a defence it must be pleaded in the defence document. This can be dealt with as a preliminary issue to prevent the time and expense of the claim running to trial only to fail on the finding that it was issued out of time. *Delaware Mansions* is the key case which sets out the limitation period in a tree root subsidence claim.

CHAPTER NINE

TPO TREES

Trees can be protected by a local planning authority (LPA) if they are within a conservation area or are protected by a tree preservation order (TPO). TPO protected trees implicated in tree root subsidence deserve a book of their own to go into detail, but this chapter sets out a summary of key points.

Where the damage to a claimant's property is caused by a TPO protected tree the options for mitigation and legal redress are complex. This is an area where civil liability, planning, statutory compensation and the Town and Country Planning Act 1990 all meet.

The Subsidence Scenario

A typical case begins when a domestic property suffers subsidence damage. Investigations may reveal cyclical patterns of seasonal movement, a hallmark of vegetation-induced damage. If roots from a nearby TPO-protected tree are recovered beneath the foundations, and engineering evidence shows that tree removal would stabilise the property, the homeowner appears to face an obvious course of action.

However, because the tree is subject to a TPO, no works can lawfully proceed without LPA consent. An application must be made, supported by detailed arboricultural and engineering evidence. The application is first validated, then determined within eight weeks. The outcome may be either approval (with or without conditions), meaning permission is given, usually valid for two years. Alternatively, a notice of refusal may be issued which is a rejection of the application, often on grounds of amenity or insufficient evidence.

Where a notice of refusal is issued the possibility of a compensation claim arises.

Statutory Basis

Compensation is governed by:

- **England:** Section 202E of the Town and Country Planning Act 1990 and Regulation 24 of the Town and Country Planning (Tree Preservation) (England) Regulations 2012.

- **Wales:** The Town and Country Planning (Trees) Regulations 1999.

The statutes provide that compensation is payable for any loss or damage suffered "in consequence of" the refusal of consent under the Regulations, or the grant of consent subject to conditions.

Principles of Compensation

Compensation is not the same as legal damages in tort; it is a statutory entitlement, with distinct limitations. The loss must satisfy the following:

- It must be the natural and probable consequence of the LPA's decision.

- It must have been within the contemplation of the LPA at the time.

- It must not be too remote.

- It must be quantifiable in monetary terms.

In practice, if refusal of consent necessitates underpinning to stabilise a house that would otherwise have been repaired cosmetically following tree removal, the cost of underpinning may form the basis of the claim.

Tribunal Jurisdiction

Compensation claims are determined by the Upper Tribunal (Lands Chamber). Importantly the claim relates only to losses caused by the refusal itself, not all expenditure on investigation or remedial works. Costs that would have been incurred regardless cannot be recovered.

Even a successful claimant is not guaranteed recovery of legal costs. There is therefore inherent risk in pursuing a claim, even if prospect of success are assessed to be strong. Rule 10 of the tribunal rules (see chapter 7) sets out information about orders for costs. There is no general entitlement to costs although the Tribunal has the discretion to make a costs order on an application or on its own initiative.

Limitation

The limitation period in a compensation claim is two-pronged and is shaped by both the terms of the tree preservation order itself and statutory limitation periods.

First is the clause from the TPO. That sets out that the Claimant has 12 months from the notice of approval to notify the LPA of the claim.

In the case of *Haringey v London Borough of Enfield (Upper Tribunal (Lands Chamber)*[26] the Tribunal was asked to consider, as a preliminary issue, whether a compensation claim had been validly made by the claimant within the statutory 12-month window. The claimant's letter

---

26 Haringey v London Borough of Enfield (Upper Tribunal (Lands Chamber) LCA/389/209

had been sent within the 12-month window. It was entitled "Notification of application for compensation". The Council argued it was a notice of intention rather than an actual claim. The Tribunal held the letter was a valid claim because although it said "intention to seek recovery" the letter clearly asserted entitlement to compensation, set out on the basis and indicated works were being carried out. A claim does not need quantified sums or full details to be valid as long as it makes it clear that compensation is being claimed.

Once the 12-month letter has been correctly served, the claimant has 6 years from the date of the Notice of Refusal to start the compensation claim off before the Lands Tribunal. This claim is started by the submission of the Notice of Reference document.

Policy Concerns for LPAs

Unlike tortious liability, where insurers can respond, LPAs have no insurance cover for TPO compensation claims. Awards are paid directly from council budgets. This creates a tension. This tension is amplified by the fact that these claims relate to high amenity trees. So, where a consent is granted for the felling of a TPO protected tree, this often attracts public attention and negative publicity.

Given the financial pressure on LPAs and the risk of compensation claims being sought against limited budgets the LPAs comment on feeling pushed to grant consent for felling, even where the tree is of high amenity value.

Possible Solutions

Several approaches may help restore balance:

- **Article 5 certificates (historic):** These exempted certain trees of exceptional value from compensation risk, but were abolished in 2012. Their reintroduction is sometimes proposed.

- **Upskilling LPAs:** Authorities should be equipped to properly assess subsidence evidence and risk, rather than relying on claimant assertions.

- **Insurance reform:** Pressure could be placed on home insurers to avoid pursuing compensation claims in TPO subsidence cases.

- **Protocols:** Agreement on using the statutory "nuisance" exemption to allow necessary works without triggering compensation.

- **Dialogue and compromise:** Open discussions between claimants and LPAs may lead to proportionate solutions short of felling.

CHAPTER TEN

COMPLAINTS TO THE FOS

A homeowner who has noticed crack damage to their property will make a claim on their home buildings insurance to get the subsidence problem remedied and the property repaired. However, there are times when an insured can get into a conflict situation with their own insurance company in the course of a tree root subsidence claim.

Where an insured and their insurer are in a conflict situation the insured should first utilise the insurance company's internal complaints process to try and reach a resolution. If that process does not reach a satisfactory conclusion from the insured following receipt of the final complaint response letter, they are able to progress their complaint to the Financial Ombudsman Service (FOS). There is a time limit of 6 months from the date of the final response letter to make the complaint to the FOS.

The FOS is the UK's independent body for resolving disputes between consumers and financial service providers. It was set up by the Financial Service and Markets Act 2000 and deals with complaints about insurers and other financial services providers.

Who can complain?

The FOS can only consider complaints from private individuals (including policyholders under domestic buildings insurance) and certain small businesses, charities, or trusts. This is not a situation in which laws of subrogation apply, insurers cannot complain in their own name.

Common Subsidence Complaints

In the context of tree root subsidence, the FOS website tells us that consumers tell them the following things in relation to subsidence:

- their insurer rejected a claim for subsidence damage because the damage wasn't caused by subsidence but by an uninsured event, such as settlement
- their claim is taking a long time to resolve
- they felt their insurer hasn't communicated with them
- their insurer didn't provide adequate alternative accommodation while repairs were being made
- their insurer proposed a claim settlement that the customer feels isn't enough, for example when the customer wants the entire property underpinned but the insurer says that less extensive remedial measures will do
- repairs completed by their insurer are poor
- repairs completed by their insurer caused further damage
- their insurer unwilling to provide continued cover following a subsidence claim

The Process

Once the complaint has been submitted (online, by email or post) the FOS will check it is within their jurisdiction and will gather information and evidence from both the consumer and the insurer. The complaint is then reviewed by an investigator who will give their view on the complaint. At this stage the insured has the option to accept or reject the investigator's outcome. If they reject the outcome they can ask for the complaint to be referred to the Ombudsman for a formal decision. The Ombudsman then makes a written decision on what is fair and reasonable depending on the facts, the law (although not bound to follow the law) and good industry practice.

If the insured accepts the Ombudsman's decision it is legally binding on the insurer. If the insured rejects the decision then they are free to utilise litigation to take their complaint forward to a Court decision.

Whilst the FOS process is underway the insured cannot issue proceedings at court at the same time. If court proceedings are issued, the FOS will stop dealing with the complaint.

Remedies

The FOS has the following remedies available to it:

- Direct the insurer to take remedial action (e.g., re-open a claim, appoint new experts, pay for alternative repairs)
- Award compensation for distress and inconvenience (typically up to £1,000)
- Award compensation for financial loss, including costs incurred due to the insurer's mishandling of the claim

The FOS can award up to £415,000 (from 1 April 2023 onwards) for complaints referred on or after that date, though the majority of subsidence-related awards are modest and focused on customer service failings rather than full indemnities.

Complain or Litigate?

Making a complaint to the FOS is free of charge and is set up for individuals to use without the need for legal representation. Some issues can be more or less suitable for a complaint to the FOS. More complex issues involving a claim for damages in excess of the £415,000 maximum and where there is legal representation and legal costs will be sought, litigation may be preferable.

Past Decisions

There is no precedent effect of past FOS decisions. However, decisions are held on the FOS website and are a useful starting point when looking to see what the FOS has decided in past, similar complaints. As there is no precedent effect and the FOS is not bound to follow law, it can be difficult to predict what the outcome of a complaint will be.

Considering past decisions, this is a good guide of what the FOS will consider:

1. Underlying causes must be dealt with – the insurer should fund remedial works that stop the subsidence continuing.

2. Standard of works – the repair must be 'lasting and effective'. The FOS expects a repair scheme that ensures the property's stability in the long term.

3. Monitoring is part of a lasting repair – the FOS recognises that a period of monitoring is reasonable before deciding on a repair scheme. However, once that has been done, the work must settle the issue for good (lasing and effective repair).

Changes from January 2026

From 2026 the relationship between the Financial Ombudsman Service (FOS) and the Financial Conduct Authority (FCA) will shift. Reforms will require the FOS to align more closely with the FCA's rules and guidance, including a formal referral mechanism for clarification where rules are unclear. The FOS's "fair and reasonable" test will be tied more explicitly to FCA compliance, and complaints will be subject to a ten-year time limit. These changes aim to reduce inconsistency and provide greater predictability for firms and consumers alike, though they also narrow the Ombudsman's discretion.

CHAPTER ELEVEN

INSURANCE COVER AND THE ABI

Where a domestic property suffers from subsidence damage, this is a peril which is covered by the buildings insurance policy. As we have covered earlier in this book, since 1976 cover for subsidence damage has largely been offered across the insurance industry.

The Association of British Insurers (ABI) is the main UK trade body which represents insurance and long-term savings companies. The ABI is not a regulator. It sets the industry positions, lobbies government, coordinates responses to issues and produces market data. Copies of the ABI Agreements relating to tree root subsidence are found on the ABI website.[27]

ABI Agreement

Tree root subsidence is a unique insurance peril in that it occurs over a period of time, unlike other perils such as fires or impact damage which happen on a given date. There can be a delay between the onset of damage at a property and that damage being noticed and reported by the policyholder. Once noticed and a claim being made, the damage can continue. We refer to the House of Lords case of *Delaware Mansions* where the House of Lords referred to an unabated nuisance being a nuisance that reoccurs every day.

[27] Association of British Insurers, abi-domestic-subsidence-claims-agreement-and-guidelines-december-2017.pdf (December 2017) and ABI DOMESTIC SUBSIDENCE TREE ROOT CLAIMS AGREEMENT (updated May 2017)

In real terms, the process of trying to abate the nuisance can take years. A key piece of evidence is the monitoring of the building and capturing the seasonal pattern of that monitoring requires it being taken over the seasons. It is common for tree owning local authorities to seek 12 months of monitoring to evidence a causal link between the movement and their tree.

In making these comments about the time frame it is important to bear in mind that insurance cover can change over time for the insured. The cost-conscious insured can swap insurers as they shop-around for a good insurance deal. In order to address the fact that these perils happen over a timeframe within which insurance cover might have switched, the ABI created the Domestic Subsidence "Change of Insurer" Claims Agreement. There are three options which are all calculated from the date of notification of the insurance claim. Those options are:

- **Option 1**: Where the Date of Notification is eight weeks or less from the date of inception of the current Insurer's policy, any claim shall be accepted and dealt with by the previous Insurer and no contribution shall be requested from the current Insurer.

- **Option 2**: Where the Date of Notification is one year or more from the date of inception of the current Insurer's policy, any claim shall be accepted and dealt with by the current Insurer and no contribution shall be requested from the previous Insurer.

- **Option 3**: Where the Date of Notification is more than eight weeks but less than one year from the date of inception of the current Insurer's policy, any claim shall be accepted and dealt with by the Insurer to whom notification is given and the Cost of Settlement shared equally between the two Insurers (50/50).

Where a subrogated claim follows the completion of a tree root subsidence claim and Option 3 applies, the current insurer manages the subrogated claim and then reimburses the previous insurer 50% of the recovery secured.

The ABI has produced a further subsidence guide, the ABI Domestic Subsidence Tree Root Claims Agreement, Third Party Liability. That agreement sets out that where tree root subsidence has been caused by a domestic tree owner, and where both the claimant householder and defendant tree owner are insured by insurers subscribing to the ABI, they agree not to pursue a recovery claim where the tree is the cause of the damage. This is limited to the first claim only and the agreement makes clear that, in the event of a recurrent or no reasonable preventative measures having taken place, the agreement will not bite if there is a subsequent claim.

Climate Change

The ABI produced their first Climate Change Roadmap in 2021, setting out milestones to be met by the insurance industry to keep the sector on track to halve emissions by 2030 and reach net zero by 2050. This roadmap was updated in 2023 and guidance on it can be found on the ABI website.

Insurance companies are increasingly aware of the environmental impact of not only their Scope 1 and 2 carbon emissions (i.e., their direct and indirect burning of fossil fuels) but they are aware of the impact of their Scope 3 emissions from their processes and supply chain.

Tree Law's Subsidence Calculator® is a carbon calculation tool which has been launched to the market and allows insurers to carbon footprint the different outcomes in a tree root subsidence claim in order to allow them to be better informed in making a reasonable decision as to which remedial route to choose. Other carbon footprinting tools also exist and these tools, as a whole, will be used to help insurers hit targets to reduce the carbon impact of the management of their tree root subsidence claims.

Disputes

Where there is a dispute between the insured and their insurer in a tree root subsidence claim, the ABI do not get involved in these disputes. Such disputes are for the Financial Ombudsman Service or the Court.

NHBC Guidance

The National House Building Council (NHBC) Standards, particularly Chapter 4.2 *Building Near Trees*, are frequently considered in subsidence claims because they set out the construction practices expected when properties are built close to trees. Insurers may look to these guidelines when assessing whether subsidence damage arises from defective design or workmanship, or whether it is genuinely attributable to the influence of trees.

Where a property has been built in breach of NHBC guidance, such as with insufficient foundation depth for shrinkable clay soils close to trees, insurers sometimes decline cover, citing poor construction as the reason. Conversely, compliance with NHBC standards can bolster an insured's position by showing that reasonable precautions were taken at the time of construction, leaving the tree as the primary cause of damage.

There is change underway in relation to Chapter 4.2 and the guidance which the NHBC will be providing in terms of foundation depth when building near trees. This is another area where climate considerations arise. The NHBC will want to strike a balance between the guidance that it gives, in order to keep new-build properties stable in the presence of trees, whilst also encouraging building near trees, encouraging planting trees near buildings and also discouraging the use of incredibly carbon dioxide intense foundation solutions.

CHAPTER TWELVE

THE FUTURE OF TREE ROOT SUBSIDENCE CLAIMS

Tree root subsidence remains one of the most technically complex insurance perils. Claims often involve far more than just the homeowner and the tree owner as the involvement of trees brings in other stakeholders who represent environmental concerns. Looking forward, this area is likely to change to reflect an increasing appreciation of trees in our urban areas and an increasing depth of our knowledge on the importance of retaining our old trees.

1. Climate change and increased risk

The impact of climate change on subsidence risk is now well established. As it was commented towards the start of this guide, subsidence is the only insured peril which is made worse by climate change but where traditionally the approach sought to solve the subsidence is tree removal, which in turn contributes to making climate change worse.

Insurers and local authorities are reporting rising claim volumes after event summers such as 2003, 2018 and 2022. At the time of writing, summer 2025 is just being declared to be another event year with £153 million paid out on subsidence claims in the first half of 2025, covering nearly 9,000 claims.

The Met Office is predicting a high frequency of dry summers over the coming decades. The targets in the Paris Agreement, limiting temperatures to 1.5 degrees Celsius above preindustrial levels, are slipping away, making the risk of impacts of climate change like heatwaves ever more likely and severe.

Tree root subsidence claims are likely to continue to be found in areas not traditionally seen as high risk for subsidence and there will be increased urgency around prevention and early intervention.

2. Technology & data

Technology and data are set to transform how subsidence claims are investigated and resolved. Advances in remote sensing, soil moisture monitoring, and satellite imagery already allow insurers and experts to track ground movement and drought stress with far greater precision than traditional site inspections alone. Large datasets, combining meteorological records, tree canopy mapping, and building age profiles, are being combined to model subsidence risk at postcode or even property level. For claimants and defendants this means causation arguments will increasingly rely on predictive analytics rather than isolated expert opinion.

3. Changes to insurance?

A reinsurance model for subsidence, similar to **Flood Re**, has been discussed as a possible insurance reform allowing insurers to manage the risk of covering this peril. The logic here is that subsidence claims increase dramatically in "surge years" leaving insurers exposed to concentrated, high-value losses and intense pressure on their supply chain. A pooled reinsurance scheme could spread that risk across the market, stabilising premiums for householders in clay-soil regions and easing pressure on individual insurers during drought cycles. This would differ from Flood:Re though. Subsidence is not just climate-driven but also linked to various factors which can make the underwriting more complex. A "Subsidence Re" would need robust data-sharing on property risk factors and an industry agreement to balance the importance of making insurance cover affordable with the private responsibilities of tree owners. While often discussed in the press it is not yet on the policy agenda and it is anticipated it will continue to be discussed, especially at times of a claims surge.

Parametric insurance is likely to play a growing role in the future of subsidence claims. Parametric policies pay out automatically when pre-agreed triggers are met, such as a certain level of soil shrinkage, ground movement detected by sensors, or extended periods of low rainfall. For homeowners this would reduce claim duration and bring certainty to what is a complex claims process. If adopted widely, parametric cover could reshape the landscape of subsidence claims from a reactive, litigation-prone model to one that is faster, data-driven, and preventative.

4. Attitude change

Attitudes to subsidence claims are likely to shift in step with wider climate commitments. The Paris Agreement has pushed governments, insurers, and local authorities to consider not just immediate financial loss but the long-term resilience of housing and urban green infrastructure. In this context, trees are increasingly valued as vital for carbon capture, cooling, and flood mitigation, meaning the old assumption that felling is the default response to subsidence may come under pressure. Future claims could be argued through a different lens, not only about private property damage, but about how to balance those losses against legally binding climate targets. Homeowners, insurers, and councils may find themselves nudged toward compromise solutions such as root barriers, foundation strengthening, or selective pruning, rather than wholesale removal of mature trees. Over time, the cultural framing of "tree versus house" may soften into a more nuanced conversation about shared responsibility.

5. Task Force on Climate Related Financial Disclosures

In the UK, TCFD reporting has already become mandatory for all insurers. From 2022, these entities have been required to disclose how climate-related risks, both physical (like subsidence, flooding, wildfires) and transitional (policy and regulatory shifts), affect their strategy and financial resilience. For subsidence, this means insurers must go beyond treating it as an occasional surge peril and explicitly map how hotter, drier summers are altering long-term exposure. As regulators and investors scrutinise these disclosures, pressure builds for insurers to show credible adaptation strategies. For the insured this could mean a more transparent explanation of insurance cover decisions, while for the wider insurance system it frames tree root subsidence as a climate risk with financial stability implications, reported at board level and benchmarked against international standards.

6. Housing Crisis

The housing crisis adds another layer of complexity to the future of tree root subsidence claims. As demand for new homes intensifies, more developments are being built on marginal land, including clay-heavy soils already prone to shrink-swell movement. At the same time, the push for higher-density housing often places new foundations closer to existing mature trees, increasing the likelihood of root-related damage. Local authorities and housing providers are under political pressure to preserve urban tree cover for climate and amenity reasons, while also delivering much-needed housing stock. Courts and tribunals could find themselves mediating not just between homeowner and tree owner, but between the competing priorities of climate resilience, affordable housing, and individual loss.

Conclusion

With global temperatures rising and 84% of the UK population living in urban areas it is never more important than now to ensure that we can live amongst our urban forest. The shade of a tree can lower temperatures by up to 10 degrees Celsius. Simply put, retaining trees in our cities and close to our properties is key to making sure we can continue to live in our cities.

As subsidence becomes a more pressing environmental and legal challenge, those handling these claims will need to remain agile, well-informed, and ready to adapt.

We hope that this Guide is helpful for lawyers involved in the management of these claims.

APPENDIX A

GLOSSARY OF DEFINITIONS

This appendix provides definitions for key legal, technical, and procedural terms used throughout this book. These definitions are provided in the context of a tree root subsidence claim.

A	
Abatement	The common law right of a landowner to take reasonable, proportionate steps to remove or prevent a nuisance, such an encroaching tree roots, without a court order.
Association of British Insurers (ABI)	The trade body representing the UK insurance industry. The ABI have 2 agreements relating to tree root subsidence.
Arboriculturalist	A tree expert specialising in the management, health and the structural stability of trees.
B	
Buildings insurance	The type of insurance that covers and protects the structure of a property. A tree root subsidence claim will be dealt with by the buildings insurer.

BRE Guide 251	Building Research Establishment Digest 251: Assessment of Damage in Low-Rise Buildings – provides a classification for structural damage to houses.
Bore hole	A hole dug into the soil in order to retrieve soil and root samples to test for causation evidence.
C	
Causation	The legal and evidential requirement to show that the defendant's action/inaction has been the primary cause of the damage alleged by the claimant.
Claimant	The owner of the property which has experienced crack damage.
Clay soil	Soil composed of fine particles that expand when wet and contract when dry. The high shrink/swell capacity of clay soils makes it prone to movement in the presence of roots.
Cracks	Tree root subsidence damage shows itself as crack damage to areas of weakness of property, such as around windows and doors.
Crack Monitoring	Monitoring of the opening and closing of cracks at a property to ascertain whether the property is moving seasonally, i.e., with cracks opening in the summer and closing in the winter.

Conservation Area	An area of special architectural or historic interest, the character or appearance of which it is desirable to preserve or enhance. Notification needs to be made to the local planning authority before work is carried out to a tree in a conservation area (section 211 application).
CAVAT	A valuation method for putting a monetary figure on the amenity value of public trees. It treats trees as community assets, factoring in size, condition, location, and the population that benefits from them.
Climate Change	The change in weather patterns caused by the change in global temperature brought about by (largely) human emissions of green house gases. Linking directly to hotter, drier summers in the UK.
Carbon Footprint	A carbon footprint is the total amount of greenhouse gases (mainly carbon dioxide, but also methane, nitrous oxide, etc.) released into the atmosphere as a result of an activity, product, service, person, or organisation. It's usually expressed as carbon dioxide equivalent (CO_2e).
Cyclical Movement	Movement of a property characteristic of tree root subsidence with the property moving downwards in the summer as the soil dries and shrinks in volume and upwards in the winter as the soil rehydrates and swells.

D	
Duty of Care	A duty of care is the legal obligation to take reasonable care to avoid acts or omissions which could reasonably be foreseen as likely to cause harm to other.
Defendant	The tree owner or the person/company/organisation with control over the tree/s implicated in the damage.
Damage	Damage caused by tree root subsidence can appear as cracks, distortions, sticking windows/doors, gaps between skirting boards and walls, fractured underground pipes.
Damages	A sum of money awarded to compensate someone for loss caused by someone else's act or omission.
Drainage	Leaking drains can be a cause of subsidence damage as water washes away the ground underneath the property foundations. A drainage inspection will confirm whether there are any leaks from the drainage system which could the cause of the damage.
Distortion Survey	A structural survey that measures and records the extent of movement or deformation in a building, usually caused by foundation movement.

Date of Notification	The date referenced by the ABI Agreement Change of Insurer Agreement.
E	
Encroachment	When roots from a tree grow across a boundary line from the tree owner's land into a neighbour's property, without permission.
Expert Evidence	Opinion evidence given by a suitable qualified person to help a Court understand technical or specialised matters. Common expert evidence in a tree root subsidence claim being engineering and arboricultural.
Engineering evidence	Technical evidence to link the damage to the property to what is happening to the ground. Including soil evidence, monitoring evidence, foundation details.
F	
FNOL	First notification of loss – the date when the insured makes the notification to their insurance company of the crack damage.
Foreseeability	The test of whether the reasonable person in the Defendant's position would have anticipated the risk of harm.

Financial Ombudsman Service (FOS)	The UK independent body set up by statute and which determines disputes between customers and insurers.
G	
Ground Movement	The change in soil volume and stability beneath the foundations of a property caused by the moisture extraction from soil by tree roots.
Guidance	Industry guidance from the Association of British Insurers, National House Building Council, Building Research Establishment, London Tree Officers' Association.
General Damages	Compensatory damages for loss which cannot be precisely calculated in monetary terms.
H	
Heave	The upward ground movement when soils rehydrate. The opposite movement to the downwards subsidence movement. The risk of damage being caused by heave can depend on whether the tree predates the property and how desiccated the soil was when the house was built. A heave survey to assess the risk of heave damage following tree removal can be carried out.

Historic Damage	Damage caused by cracking or movement which has occurred in the past and is not progressive.
Housing Associations	Institutional landowners who can regularly appear in tree root subsidence claims, largely due to their volume of property ownership across the UK.
I	
Injunction	A court order requiring a party to do an act or prevent a party from acting. For example an order to compel a tree owner to remove a tree.
Insured Loss	Financial loss of the insurance company who have managed the tree root subsidence claim and which they seek to recover from a liable third party via the subrogated recovery claim. The loss must be within the terms and conditions of the contract of insurance. A voluntary payment made by the insurer to their insured does not form a recoverable insured loss.
Innovation	The process of developing and applying new ideas, technologies and methods, to improve how something is done.

J	
Joint Mitigation Protocol	A voluntary agreement between insurance companies and local authority tree owners setting out a cooperative process for the handling of tree root subsidence claims, in particular focusing on mitigation.
Joint Experts	Where a claim is in litigation the parties can agree, or be ordered by the Court, to instruct a joint expert in a given field. The use of joint experts can also be ordered by the FOS to assist in the determination of a dispute between customer and insurer.
K	
Knowledge	Whether a defendant knew, or ought to have known, about a risk is important in order to determine foreseeability.
L	
Limitation	The time limit, set out by the Limitation Act 1980, within which proceedings need to be started at Court otherwise the legal claim is statue barred, i.e., out of time, and can no longer progress.

Lands Tribunal	The Court to whom claims for compensation are brought pursuant to S202E of the Town and Country Planning Act 1990 following refusal of permission to fell a TPO protected tree.
Local Planning Authority	The council who manages tree preservation orders and conservations. The body to whom a planning application for permission to work on a tree in a CA or a TPO protected tree should be made.
M	
Mitigation	The duty on the claimant to take reasonable steps to lessen their loss after harm as occurred.
Monitoring	Crack of level monitoring commonly carried out in tree root subsidence cases. This is the process of measuring movement of a property over time to determine if the pattern of movement shows cyclical movement, characteristic of tree root subsidence.
Mediation	A voluntary and without prejudice meeting, facilitated by an independent mediator, to reach a compromise in a dispute between parties.

N	
Negligence	The failure to exercise reasonable care, leading to loss or damage.
Nuisance	Unlawful interference with a person's use or enjoyment of their land.
NHBC	National House Building Council, sets standards and provides warranties for new home. Guidance includes foundation depth when building near trees.
P	
Pre Action Protocol	The Practice Direction on Pre Action Conduct and Protocols which sets out the pre action process the Court expect the parties to adhere to in a case prior to litigation. Relevant to tree root subsidence litigation.
Paris Agreement	An international 2015 treaty aiming to limit global warming to well below 2°C, with efforts to keep it to 1.5°C, through national carbon dioxide emission reduction commitments.

R	
Root Barrier	A physical barrier/membrane installed in the ground to restrict the spread of tree roots from one area to another.
Resin Injection	A ground improvement technique where expanding resin is injected into soil beneath property to fill voids.
Replanting	Where permission is given to fell a tree protected by a TPO, it will be a requirement to replant a tree to replace the tree which has been lost. Increasingly, offers to replant trees (not TPO protected) is being made as part of tree root subsidence cases.
S	
Subsidence	The downward movement of ground supporting a building causing the foundations of that building to move.
Subrogation	The right of an insurer, after making a payment under a contact of insurance, to step into the shoes of their insured to pursue a recovery from a responsible third party.
Satellite Monitoring	The use of satellite imagery to detect or measure ground or structural movement over time.

Shrink/Swell	The characteristic of a clay soil, shrinking in volume as it dries out and swelling in volume as it rehydrates.
T	
Tree Preservation Order	An order placed on a tree by a Local Planning Authority which gives it protection. An application needs to be made to the LPA before work can be carried out to the tree unless one of the exemptions to protection applies.
Trial Pit	A small, excavated hole dug close to a building to uncover the foundations and underlying soil.
U	
Uninsured Losses	Financial losses incurred by an insured homeowner which are not paid by their insurance company pursuant to the contract of insurance.
Underpinning	A method of strengthening and stabilising a building's foundations, usually by extending them to a deeper or more stable soil layer.

APPENDIX B

KEY CASE LAW IN TREE ROOT SUBSIDENCE CLAIMS

A very short summary of the key point arising from each case is provided. Please read the cases in full in order to understand the judgment.

Lemmon v Webb [1895]	Confirmed that a landowner may lawfully cut encroaching vegetation back to the boundary without notice, establishing the principle of self-help abatement in nuisance cases.
Bunclark v Hertfordshire County Council [1977]	Established that a tree owner can be liable for subsidence damage if they *ought reasonably* to have foreseen the risk, even without actual knowledge.
Leakey v National Trust [1980]	Held that landowners are liable in nuisance if they fail to take reasonable steps to prevent naturally occurring hazards, even without creating them.
Solloway v Hampshire County Council [1981]	Confirmed that a local authority could be liable for tree root subsidence where damage from its trees was reasonably foreseeable and no reasonable preventative action was taken.

Greenwood v Portwood [1985]	Decided that a tree owner was liable for subsidence damage because the risk from the species and soil type was reasonably foreseeable, even without actual knowledge.
Patterson v Humberside County Council [1995]	Clarified that even if trees are located some distance from the damaged property, liability can arise if the roots extend far enough to cause foreseeable damage.
Delaware Mansions Ltd v Westminster City Council [2002]	Established that a landowner who knows, or ought to know, that their tree is causing subsidence must take reasonable steps to abate the nuisance, even if the damage began before they acquired the property.
LE Jones v Portsmouth City Council [2002]	Confirmed that a local authority was liable for tree root subsidence where it failed to act once it ought reasonably to have known its trees were causing damage.
Malewski v Ealing Council [2003]	Held the council liable for subsidence damage from its tree roots, reaffirming that foreseeability of risk and failure to act reasonably are enough to establish nuisance.
Siddiqui v Hillingdon [2003]	Reaffirmed that moderate damage may still give rise to liability and that the threshold for nuisance is not limited to severe or dangerous movement.

Loftus Brigham v Ealing [2003]	Confirmed that a council was liable for tree root subsidence where it failed to take timely action once the risk of damage from its trees was, or should have been, appreciated.
Gerard-Reynolds v Brent [2005]	Held the council liable for tree root subsidence after finding it had sufficient knowledge of the risk and failed to take reasonable preventative action.
Kirk v Brent [2005]	Found the council liable for tree root subsidence because the damage was reasonably foreseeable and no adequate steps were taken to prevent it.
Hilda's Montessori Nursery Limited v Tesco [2006]	Held Tesco liable for subsidence damage caused by tree roots on its land, as the risk was foreseeable and it failed to act reasonably to prevent the nuisance.
Eiles v London Borough of Southwark [2006]	Confirmed that a claimant could recover general damages for loss of amenity and enjoyment of property in addition to the cost of repairing subsidence damage caused by tree roots.
Raphael v Brent [2007]	The court found that delay in implementing recommended tree management measures was sufficient to constitute unreasonable conduct in nuisance.

Park v Swindon [2011]	A case highlighting the need for prompt action once causation is established; repeated postponement of tree removal contributed to worsening damage.
Berent v Family Mosaic Housing & Islington LBC [2012]	Held that subsidence damage was not foreseeable in a "hot spot" area without specific warning signs, limiting liability where the risk could not reasonably have been anticipated.
Robbins v Bexley LBC [2012]	Held the council liable for tree root subsidence, confirming that once on notice of a real risk, a landowner must take reasonable steps to prevent further damage.
Denness v East Hampshire [2012]	Demonstrated that even partial root encroachment can trigger liability if the roots materially contribute to the damage.
Khan v Harrow & Kane [2013]	Confirmed that a tree owner could be liable for subsidence damage where it was reasonably foreseeable that their tree posed a risk, even without actual knowledge of the problem.
Pattichis v Enfield [2016]	Showed that historic subsidence incidents involving the same tree can be used to establish foreseeability in future claims.

Ridge v Westminster [2016]	Held the council liable for subsidence damage from its tree roots, reaffirming the duty to act once the risk of damage is, or ought to be, appreciated.
Gurdwara v Kensington [2019]	Addressed causation of damage and the reasonableness of repair works. The Court finding that there may have been another reason behind the demolition and rebuild works.
Kimeze Mpanga v London Borough of Ealing [2021]	County Court dismissed the homeowners against the council, holding that the action was statute-barred and, even if it had not been, the council had taken reasonable care in inspecting and maintaining the tree so no liability arose

APPENDIX C

KEY CASE LAW IN TPO COMPENSATION CLAIMS

A very short summary of the key point arising from each case is provided. Please read the cases in full in order to understand the judgment.

Mooney v West Lindsey District Council LCA/98/1999	The Lands Tribunal awarded £5,739 plus interest after finding limited recoverable costs following an unreasonable refusal to fell protected trees, rejecting large claims for loss of earnings and stress as unsubstantiated and excessive.
Duncan & Prudential Assurance v Epping Forest District Council LCA/62/2003	The Lands Tribunal held that compensation could be claimed for a deemed refusal of consent to fell TPO trees, but only extra costs caused by the refusal (not pre-existing damage) and reasonable appeal costs were recoverable.
Woodhams v Chichester District Council LCA/167/2006	The Lands Tribunal dismissed a claim for compensation over refusal to fell a TPO oak, holding there was no proof the tree caused or risked subsidence, so alleged blight and loss of insurance did not justify an award.

Keates v Haringey Council LCA/389/209	The Upper Tribunal held that a solicitor's letter sent within the 12-month limit, though phrased as an intention to claim, was enough to constitute a valid claim for TPO compensation, so the reference was not time-barred.
Wright & Aviva Insurance Limited v Horsham District Council LA/509/2010	The Upper Tribunal awarded £24,001.25 compensation (including distress) after refusal to fell TPO oaks, holding that the trees caused subsidence, underpinning was the natural and foreseeable consequence of refusal, and would not have been required if felling had been allowed.
Halifax General Insurance Service v Teignbridge District Council LCA/288/2010	The Upper Tribunal awarded £7,602 compensation after refusal to crown reduce a TPO oak, finding evidence showed the tree caused subsidence and that underpinning works were a reasonable, cost-effective response.
Grammar School of John Lyon v City of Westminster LCA/41/2011	The Upper Tribunal awarded £68,511.58 plus interest after refusal to fell a TPO robinia, holding it caused foreseeable subsidence at the adjoining property and underpinning was a reasonable and proportionate response.

Burge v South Gloucestershire Council LCA/105/2015	The Upper Tribunal awarded £25,000 compensation after refusal to fell a TPO oak, holding that the tree's roots caused foreseeable subsidence damage to the claimants' conservatory and that the council failed to show the loss was due to inadequate construction.
Chubb European v Enfield Council LCA/2024/52	The Upper Tribunal dismissed a £143k compensation claim for underpinning after refusal to fell a TPO oak, holding the insurer failed to prove on the balance of probabilities that the tree caused the subsidence, with alternative explanations like drainage failure more likely.

MORE BOOKS BY LAW BRIEF PUBLISHING

A selection of our other titles available now:-

'The Electronic Communications Code: A Practical Guide – Second Edition' by Kerry Bretherton KC, James Castle, Mark Loveday
'A Practical Guide to the Independent School Standards – September 2023 Edition' by Sarah McKimm
'A Practical Guide to Estate Administration and Crypto Assets' by Richard Marshall
'A Practical Guide to Parental Alienation in Private and Public Law Children Cases' by Sam King QC & Frankie Shama
'Contested Heritage – Removing Art from Land and Historic Buildings' by Richard Harwood QC, Catherine Dobson, David Sawtell
'The Limits of Separate Legal Personality: When Those Running a Company Can Be Held Personally Liable for Losses Caused to Third Parties Outside of the Company' by Dr Mike Wilkinson
'A Practical Guide to Transgender Law' by Robin Moira White & Nicola Newbegin
'A Practical Guide to 'Stranded Spouses' in Family Law' by Mani Singh Basi
'A Practical Guide to Residential Freehold Conveyancing' by Lorraine Richardson
'A Practical Guide to Pensions on Divorce for Lawyers' by Bryan Scant
'A Practical Guide to Challenging Sham Marriage Allegations in Immigration Law' by Priya Solanki
'A Practical Guide to Digital Communications Evidence in Criminal Law' by Sam Willis
'A Practical Guide to Legal Rights in Scotland' by Sarah-Jane Macdonald
'A Practical Guide to New Build Conveyancing' by Paul Sams & Rebecca East
'A Practical Guide to Inherited Wealth on Divorce' by Hayley Trim
'A Practical Guide to Practice Direction 12J and Domestic Abuse in Private Law Children Proceedings' by Rebecca Cross & Malvika Jaganmohan
'A Practical Guide to Confiscation and Restraint' by Narita Bahra QC, John Carl Townsend, David Winch
'A Practical Guide to the Law of Forests in Scotland' by Philip Buchan
'A Practical Guide to Health and Medical Cases in Immigration Law' by Rebecca Chapman & Miranda Butler
'A Practical Guide to Bad Character Evidence for Criminal Practitioners by Aparna Rao
'A Practical Guide to Extradition Law post-Brexit' by Myles Grandison et al
'A Practical Guide to Hoarding and Mental Health for Housing Lawyers' by Rachel Coyle

'Stephens on Contractual Indemnities' by Richard Stephens

'A Practical Guide to the EU Succession Regulation' by Richard Frimston

'A Practical Guide to Solicitor and Client Costs – Second Edition' by Robin Dunne

'Constructive Dismissal – Practice Pointers and Principles' by Benjimin Burgher

'A Practical Guide to Religion and Belief Discrimination Claims in the Workplace' by Kashif Ali

'A Practical Guide to the Law of Medical Treatment Decisions' by Ben Troke

'Fundamental Dishonesty and QOCS in Personal Injury Proceedings: Law and Practice' by Jake Rowley

'A Practical Guide to the Law in Relation to School Exclusions' by Charlotte Hadfield & Alice de Coverley

'A Practical Guide to Divorce for the Silver Separators' by Karin Walker

'The Right to be Forgotten – The Law and Practical Issues' by Melissa Stock

'A Practical Guide to Planning Law and Rights of Way in National Parks, the Broads and AONBs' by James Maurici QC, James Neill et al

'A Practical Guide to Election Law' by Tom Tabori

'A Practical Guide to the Law in Relation to Surrogacy' by Andrew Powell

'A Practical Guide to Claims Arising from Fatal Accidents – Second Edition' by James Patience

'A Practical Guide to Asbestos Claims' by Jonathan Owen & Gareth McAloon

'A Practical Guide to Stamp Duty Land Tax in England and Northern Ireland' by Suzanne O'Hara

'A Practical Guide to the Law of Farming Partnerships' by Philip Whitcomb

'A Practical Guide to the Law of Unlawful Eviction and Harassment – Second Edition' by Stephanie Lovegrove

'A Practical Guide to Costs in Personal Injury Claims – Second Edition' by Matthew Hoe

'A Practical Guide to the General Data Protection Regulation (GDPR) – Second Edition' by Keith Markham

'A Practical Guide to Working with Litigants in Person and McKenzie Friends in Family Cases' by Stuart Barlow

'Protecting Unregistered Brands: A Practical Guide to the Law of Passing Off' by Lorna Brazell

'A Practical Guide to Secondary Liability and Joint Enterprise Post-Jogee' by Joanne Cecil & James Mehigan

'A Practical Guide to the Pre-Action RTA Claims Protocol for Personal Injury Lawyers' by Antonia Ford

'A Practical Guide to Neighbour Disputes and the Law' by Alexander Walsh

'A Practical Guide to Coercive Control for Legal Practitioners and Victims' by Rachel Horman

'A Practical Guide to the Law of Driverless Cars – Second Edition'

by Alex Glassbrook, Emma Northey & Scarlett Milligan

'A Practical Guide to TOLATA Claims' by Greg Williams

'A Practical Guide to Elderly Law – Second Edition' by Justin Patten

'A Practical Guide to Responding to Housing Disrepair and Unfitness Claims' by Iain Wightwick

'A Practical Guide to the Law of Bullying and Harassment in the Workplace' by Philip Hyland

'How to Be a Freelance Solicitor: A Practical Guide to the SRA-Regulated Freelance Solicitor Model' by Paul Bennett

'A Practical Guide to Prison Injury Claims' by Malcolm Johnson

'A Practical Guide to Advising Clients at the Police Station' by Colin Stephen McKeown-Beaumont

'A Practical Guide to Antisocial Behaviour Injunctions – Second Edition' by Iain Wightwick

'Practical Mediation: A Guide for Mediators, Advocates, Advisers, Lawyers, and Students in Civil, Commercial, Business, Property, Workplace, and Employment Cases' by Jonathan Dingle with John Sephton

'The Mini-Pupillage Workbook' by David Boyle

'A Practical Guide to Crofting Law' by Brian Inkster

'A Practical Guide to the Law of Domain Names and Cybersquatting' by Andrew Clemson

'A Practical Guide to the Law of Gender Pay Gap Reporting' by Harini Iyengar

'NHS Whistleblowing and the Law' by Joseph England

'Employment Law and the Gig Economy' by Nigel Mackay & Annie Powell

'A Practical Guide to Noise Induced Hearing Loss (NIHL) Claims' by Andrew Mckie, Ian Skeate, Gareth McAloon

'An Introduction to Beauty Negligence Claims – A Practical Guide for the Personal Injury Practitioner' by Greg Almond

'Intercompany Agreements for Transfer Pricing Compliance' by Paul Sutton

'Zen and the Art of Mediation' by Martin Plowman

'A Practical Guide to Adoption for Family Lawyers' by Graham Pegg

'A Practical Guide to Industrial Disease Claims' by Andrew Mckie & Ian Skeate
'A Practical Guide to Conducting a Sheriff Court Proof' by Andrew Stevenson
'A Practical Guide to Vicarious Liability' by Mariel Irvine
'A Practical Guide to Applications for Landlord's Consent and Variation of Leases' by Mark Shelton
'A Practical Guide to Relief from Sanctions Post-Mitchell and Denton' by Peter Causton
'A Practical Guide to Equity Release for Advisors' by Paul Sams
'A Practical Guide to Financial Services Claims' by Chris Hegarty
'A Practical Guide to Financial Ombudsman Service Claims' by Adam Temple & Robert Scrivenor
'A Practical Guide to Running Housing Disrepair and Cavity Wall Claims – Second Edition' by Andrew Mckie & Ian Skeate
'A Practical Guide to Holiday Sickness Claims – Second Edition' by Andrew Mckie & Ian Skeate
'Arguments and Tactics for Personal Injury and Clinical Negligence Claims' by Dorian Williams
'A Practical Guide to Drone Law' by Rufus Ballaster, Andrew Firman, Eleanor Clot
'On Experts: CPR35 for Lawyers and Experts' by David Boyle
'An Introduction to Personal Injury Law' by David Boyle

These books and more are available to order online direct from the publisher at www.lawbriefpublishing.com, where you can also read free sample chapters. For any queries, call us on 0844 587 2383 or email us at mail@lawbriefpublishing.com.

Our books are all generally in stock at www.amazon.co.uk with free next day delivery for Prime members, and at good legal bookshops such as Wildy & Sons.

We are regularly launching new books in our series of practical day-to-day practitioners' guides. Visit our website and join our free newsletter to be kept informed and to receive special offers, free chapters, etc.

You can also follow us on Twitter at www.twitter.com/lawbriefpub.

www.ingramcontent.com/pod-product-compliance
Lightning Source LLC
LaVergne TN
LVHW022102200926
848481LV00003B/1045
9781918241051